THE MEANING OF WORSHIP

The Meaning of Worship

THE LYMAN BEECHER LECTURES FOR 1958

DOUGLAS HORTON

HARPER & BROTHERS, PUBLISHERS, NEW YORK

THE MEANING OF WORSHIP

Library of Congress catalog card number: 59–7151

CONTENTS

V. ECUMENICITY

FOREWORD

The Lyman Beecher Lectureship was established in 1872 by a gift from Mr. Henry W. Sage, then of Brooklyn, New York. A benefactor of Cornell University and of other educational and philanthropic institutions, Mr. Sage was a great admirer of his minister, Henry Ward Beecher. Mr. Sage wished to endow a lectureship to bring eminent preachers and ministerial students together. It is rumored that Mr. Sage wished to name the lectureship for Henry Ward Beecher, but that the great Brooklyn preacher asked that it be named instead for his father, the Reverend Lyman Beecher, a graduate of Yale, who had served a most distinguished career as a pastor and theological educator— though perhaps he is even better known as the father of his illustrious children. A story holds that Henry Ward Beecher replied to the proposal that the lectureship be named for him by saying, "No, name it for my father. At his best he was greater than all his children put together."

Henry Ward Beecher himself delivered the first three series of the Yale lectures on preaching. Since that time, year by year in almost unbroken procession, the Beecher Lectureship has brought to the Yale community the greatest preachers of the English-speaking world. This present series of Beecher Lectures is the eighty-eighth in this long succession. Of the eighty-eight, seventy-six have been published.

In introducing the 1957 lecturer, Dr. D. T. Niles of Ceylon, I said that the Beecher Lectureship over the years has shown a marked partiality for the preachers of Boston and of Scotland. In 1958 we returned to that great tradition, if by grace Cambridge may be included in the select neighborhood of Boston.

Though he was our neighbor in a pastorate in Middletown for ten years, and has paid many rather fleeting visits to the Yale Divinity School, Douglas Horton has spent most of his time jumping over us. Born in Brooklyn, he went right through New Haven to Hartford Seminary. After pastorates in Connecticut and Massachusetts, he soared overhead to a distinguished church in Chicago. Then, after seventeen years in New York and the remainder of the inhabited world as chief executive officer of the Congregational Christian Churches, he vaulted over us again to the deanship of Harvard Divinity School. In view of these many excursions past us into outer space, we were especially happy to have Dean Horton land squarely in our midst for a few days.

Dean Horton is known around the world as one of the leaders of Congregationalism and of the ecumenical movement. Despite his intensive participation in these important activities, he has maintained across the years a quiet life of scholarship. Author of half a dozen books, he also distinguished himself as one of the first to translate Barth into English. In 1928 *The Word of God and the Word of Man* appeared in translation by Douglas Horton. He has recently completed a translation from the Latin of John Norton's *Responsio,* published in June, 1958.

We hail Dean Horton as fellow seminarian, scholar, teacher, leader in church affairs. But we welcome him also as preacher and pastor, one who through many years has been able to lead people in worship and praise of the living God. His Beecher Lectures are on that theme, the exact title being "The Meaning of Worship."

LISTON POPE
Dean, Yale Divinity School

PREFACE

In these few lectures I propose to consider certain aspects of one of the strangest facts of human existence: worship. From first to last I shall look at it through the eyes of a Christian, for it is Christian worship only that I know personally, and to it alone I can bear witness. This will not, however, preclude frequent glances into non-Christian areas. I shall speak first of the sacramental experience that is likely to come to any person in Christendom, that great area which includes the Christian Church and all the culture which is influenced, even indirectly, by the church; then go on to refer to the church itself, and so to the worship that is found there, finally applying the relationships which are intrinsic to worship as a touchstone to the church's life.

What is more fascinating than the phenomenon of worship, which is to be discovered in one form or another, quaint or sophisticated, often attractive, sometimes repulsive, but invariably arresting, in every land and among all conditions of men? The Roman Cicero, who knew his world well, says that in his observation there is no nation, "however polished and educated or however brutal and barbarous," which does not believe that the gods make known their will to men in some way or other. The Greek Plutarch is also taken with the universality of the religious life:

9

If you go through the world you may find cities without walls, without letters, without rulers, without houses, without money, without theaters and games: but there has never yet been seen, nor shall be seen by man, a single city without temples and gods . . . nay, I am of opinion that a city might be sooner built without any ground beneath it than a commonwealth could be constituted altogether destitute of belief in the gods; or being constituted could be preserved. [Against Colotes. XXXI.]

Today there are highly rationalistic sectors of our own society in which religious practice has no place; there is Russia; and there are possibly other groups of human beings willing to advertise their nonreligiousness. The fact that even the most Sartrian existentialist seems to face life positively, however, writing with zest treatises that reason that no zest in life is reasonable, makes one think there are vestiges of religious faith to be found even where there are no religious practices. The notable care taken by pessimists like Schopenhauer to preserve their health has some parallel in the concern of the Russian government to maintain itself in a world where, according to what we are told of its philosophy, there are no values worth maintaining. The Soviet leaders seem to worship something. It is quite possible that we have a false understanding of their philosophy, but in any case there seem to be affirmative and religious elements in it; and certainly in all of the so-called nonreligious areas today there are enough sudden converts to the religious point of view to permit us to join Cicero and Plutarch in their acceptance of the general religiousness of the race.

Worship is a strange phenomenon because no one could sit down and draw the conclusion from consciousness in general that it belongs to man to be religious, that men *ought* to be religious. There is no reason for it; but as Kierkegaard says, all reasoning is from existence and not to existence, and the need to worship just happens, as it were, to be one of the facts of the existence of many people. I use the phrase "just happens" as I might say that God *just happens* to be God, that is, that we ourselves had nothing to do with His being what He is and have only to accept Him. This leads us to the first of the relationships discoverable in worship.

D. H.

I. Worship as Response

to a Divine Invasion

1. WORSHIP NOT A MEANS BUT AN END

Worship is an end in itself. In worship I am not busied with a means to something else. I am not then making money for the sake of something on which I may later spend it; not then striving for position of one sort or another for the sake of enlarging my influence or gaining some fulcrum whence to move my world; not then even wrestling with the thinkers of the past and their books for the sake of consolidating my thought. By worship one is delivered from that wheel of existence which ordinary motivation seems to produce. Stop almost any man hurrying at noon across the corner of Church and Elm Streets. "Why are you hurrying?" "I want to get to lunch." "Why to lunch?" "In order to eat." "Why eat?" "In order to have some strength." "Why strength?" "In order to get my work done." "Why work?" "In order to make some money." "Why money?" "In order to buy food." "Why food?" "In order to have some strength." And so on, full circle after full circle. Worship, at least, is not like that. When I try to worship for the sake of some remuneration that may accrue, worship ceases to be worship, for then it begins to use God as a means to something else. One worships God purely for the sake of worshiping God.

No human being invented worship. At least every Christian worshiper—and perhaps every true worshiper—knows that wor-

15

ship is a response to an experience originally brought to him. He does not take up the fact of God as one among several possibilities, nor does he regard bowing before Him as an interesting pastime which he has devised for himself. Always the initiative lies with deity; and though we sometimes speak of discovering God, He is always discovered as the discoverer of ourselves.

> I sought the Lord, and afterward I knew
> He moved my soul to seek him, seeking me;
> It was not I that found, O Saviour true:
> No, I was found of thee.

The preposterousness of inventing a god to worship was clearly in the mind of Talleyrand when the theophilanthropist LaRévellière-Lépeaux reported to him his disappointment at his failure to establish his new rationalistic religion of benevolence. He complained that his propaganda seemed to be making little headway.

The ex-bishop politely condoled with him, feared it was indeed a difficult task to found a new religion, more difficult than could be imagined, so difficult that he hardly knew what to advise! "Still"— so he went on after a moment's reflection—"there is one plan which you might at least try; I should recommend you to be crucified and rise again the third day."

The very idea that human contrivance has anything whatever to do with the source of worship is repugnant to the worshiper: in worship he responds to God and God alone.

There are those who say that we worship because our friends and neighbors, that is, those who control our environment, do so. Our parents, in especial, are held responsible for our custom of worship. They are thought to have imparted the habit to us with such perfection of pedagogy that it is now lodged in our lives as a veritable appetite from which we cannot depart. That the forms we use in worship, the shape our symbols take, have been dictated by the influences of environment, few would gainsay. I take it that not many of us here can enjoy public worship fully and deeply except when it is in the English language, our mother tongue. A whole worshiping congregation may be carried to the throne of Christ by one of those rare ministers of his who has the grace to pray with the tongue of angels, alike beyond the grooved pattern of the past and beyond the trite manner of the street, only when both the minister and the people are children of the same culture. But this is to say only that the lamps of worship come from the environment—not the light itself. The argument that worship as such comes to us from, let us say, our forebears, is a somewhat feeble one, for if you follow the line of succession back you must eventually in the prehistoric twilight come upon a first anthropic ancestor who started the chain. You have here the dilemma of Lucretius, who, though he could describe with glowing imagination how the world developed in a sheer mechanical way, one atom displacing another and forming new shapes in evolutionary sequence, could never quite explain on this basis how that first atom was displaced. Some Cain, some Abel in the hidden past had the bright idea of bringing an offering to the Lord in worship. Why did he do that? Why did he not act like any other member of the animal kingdom and go about his hunting, eating, sleeping, and courtship without reference to deity? The etiology of the situation demands a better answer than is given in the reference to parental instruction or to any environmental source.

Worship often surprises the human mind, coming to it not at all in a decent episcopal succession but with sudden anabaptist spontaneity. There is in New England a humanistic church in which, according to the irreverent, the name of God has not been heard since the sexton spilt some hot lead on his hand. Something should be said for that sexton: he was at least not insincere; he spoke with feeling; his words were not formalistic and empty. Perhaps we might say that he went down justified, as many a man does not who goes to church and utters the name of God simply because his neighbors do or because he has it before him to read from a book or from his memory. Now expletives, as we know, if they are said in earnest, are forced to the lips in moments of crisis—and it is interesting that at such a time it is usually the name of God that escapes the barrier of one's teeth. I cannot call the use of profanity worship, but if it did not have vestiges of worship in it, it would not be pro-fane; and its way of bursting out in an unexpected situation is a mark of its kinship to worship, which often has a similar kind of origin.

The appeal to deity is as it were forced to the lips as to the mind when the universe surprises or lays unwonted pressure upon one. Take the matter not at the individual and selfish level but at that of concern for someone else. Recall the passage in Tolstoy's classic, *Anna Karenina,* in which the hero of the tale, if it can be said to have a hero, finds himself outside the room in which his wife is in pangs of pain and may be even at the point of giving up her life. Levin, in whom the author is depicting his own life in one of its phases, and who is a professed agnostic, paces up and down in desperation, calling out, "God have mercy, pardon and help us!" Being of a philosophical turn of mind, he catches himself in an ambiguous position: rationally he knows or thinks he knows that he ought not to be lifting up any prayer whatever, but actually his real self is in the prayer rather than in his reflection concerning the inappropriateness if it.

Our divinity schools during the last ten years have had in them not a few men who in their battle careers in the armed services were surprised into worship. Though without training in the things of religion, they were not without sensitivity, and as a result the uncovering of a life-and-death need for God in the midst of a situation of stark reality came to them as an unanticipated revelation. Never before in history have the schools of this type received so many applications from prospective ministers who fill in the line where they are to name the denomination in which they have been born and bred with the word: "None." The number of such prospective students is not large, to be sure, but there are enough to indicate that worship does not necessarily come to a man through his ancestry, spiritual or physical.

That God is creator is nowhere more surely indicated than in the religious life itself. It is God who lays His hand to the dust of our experience, and man miraculously becomes a living soul —and knows it, and wants to worship.

2. GOD ESTABLISHES A PERSON-TO-PERSON RELATIONSHIP

He Comes as a Question and as the Answer

When God speaks in one of those experiences which can perhaps best be called sacramental—when He steps out of the bright, variegated shadow which is the world and makes Himself known—it is to a human soul that He presents Himself. The experience is always fiercely personal. When you truly encounter Him, it is not as a chance passer-by, from whom you may turn away without ado. You do not make a lighthearted decision to recognize Him or not to do so. Once you are aware of Him you are more likely to take up the Psalmist's moan, "Whither shall I go from thy spirit, or whither shall I flee from thy presence?" When *He* speaks, His words reach their hearer, even if he be an over-hearer. It is easier to take nonchalantly the lightning that strikes near you than God.

Often, as we know, the first experience of religion is in the form of searching. This is normal in contemporary Christianity. Indeed, for Christians the Gospel never loses this ingredient, though as the life of worship matures, the element of finding is more and more recognized and clasped to the soul.

Within Christendom the experience of being worried by a question, by a nameless principle of existence, must be taken for granted. This it is which is delineated in so many different ways by our contemporary existentialists. It is so universal that it is often called the human dilemma, as characteristic of the human situation. I do not think, however, that the name "human" is the best to apply to it. For one reason, we cannot know that it is actually characteristic of the entire human race. There may be exceptions, especially outside the area where the Gospel has been preached. But the fundamental reason for not calling it human is because the many human beings in whom the strange questioning about existence has arisen have recognized it as coming from outside. It is not their idea. They have been disturbed by it from the direction of outer existence. I think of it therefore not as a human piece of business but as the work of God's Holy Spirit, broadly operative upon most of us, and disturbing to most.

The experience of dimly felt first-revelation is not only a question. It is a sense of being demanded. The soft unceasing steps of the Hound of Heaven begin to be heard. There is resistance to being overtaken, but this loses its power as the divine requisition makes itself known. Of such an experience C. S. Lewis writes:

> I had always wanted, above all things, not to be "interfered with." . . . You must picture me alone in that room in Magdalen, night after night, feeling, whenever my mind lifted even for a second from my work, the steady, unrelenting approach of him whom I desired so earnestly not to meet.

His chapter giving the entire description of the event carries under its title a quotation from George MacDonald: "The one principle of hell is—'I am my own.'" (And the name of the book, which seems in itself to illustrate what I have been saying, is, as you will recall, *Surprised by Joy*.)

The question felt by Christians presently opens into an answer, the demand into a sense of being supplied. Here paradox rules. The very search for God already includes a finding of Him. It is a sweet and lovely hour when one awakens to this truth. Auguste Sabatier on coming upon it in Pascal felt himself to have discovered a key to the meaning of existence. Pascal, meditating upon Christ, had with the ears of the spirit heard him say to him, "Thou wouldst not seek me hadst thou not already found me." Yes: if you were an animal, as some have said that you are, or a vegetable, as others incline to hold, or a congeries of atoms swirling about in the interesting configuration we call a human being, and nothing more, one would think that the mere law of momentum would hold you in contentment to your animalhood, your vegetableness, or your atomicity. Why should a mere animal want to be anything but an animal? The very fact that you ask after something else is an indication that something else has touched you at the heart of your being. Who would seek Christ whom Christ had not found? All this is nothing if not personal. It is not an argument convincing in itself; it is only an attempt to give a rationale for an experience which you may have had: when hunger for God comes out of personal depth, it contains by paradox a quantum of correspondingly deep satisfaction.

Here lies the fascination of such authors as Kafka and Camus. Superficially, their kind of existentialism seems the very nadir of the negative. Life is confusion, uncertainty: no questions are answered. Why then do so many good Christian readers find their writings so compelling? Take *The Castle* or *The Plague,* for instance.

A man comes to a city to do a piece of work; he is ready and eager to begin, and as he has to know what is wanted of him, he starts searching for the one who can tell him—up in the castle which dominates the city. The search goes on: he never finds him. A doctor without any formal faith whatever delivers a city from a plague while the people who conceive themselves believers are victims of their own fears, only clog the enterprise with their futility, and, once the dreadful blight has passed, relapse into light, semi-happy, and even religious routine. What comfort is there for serious-minded Christians in this? The answer is that an unseen affirmation lies within the seen negation. It is something that the man who has come to the city knows he has a piece of work to do. It is something that the doctor, if blindly, knows that he has to do his best to save the community. He is more of a religious personality, responding more sensitively to a governing will beyond his own and beyond humanity's own, than the more showily but shallowly religious people of the tale. For such a lesson we may wisely go to school to the existentialists.

Sooner or later, however, the experience of God as the one

and only answer to the question and the felt demand of the existence He has given us must come to its maturity and be recognized and embraced. God is not understood in His fullness until, responding to Him, we know Him as the answer. The sacramental experience turns into personal worship when I realize that God is present, and that I am not asking Him a question to which He may give an answer but that He *is* the answer to the deepest longing of my soul. In Him we come to realize we are at home. Everywhere else we are separated from the place whence we derived our lives and to which we long to return, but here we are at the very matrix of existence. Here, in true worship, is that mutuality of knowing which is hidden in the old Hebrew word *yada*, "know," which always implies some kind of contact. Here we are in contact with the essence of life and the essence of life is in contact with us. Living as I do usually in a far country I have said, "I will arise and go to my father"; and now I have come to him and been received not as a hired servant but as a son of the family.

Worship is realized as the maintenance of a primordial relationship between yourself and the sources of your self's life roughly analogous to the relationship between flower and sunshine, the thinking mind and truth. You cannot get along without it. It comes to you as a kind of demand but as a demand with which your whole being collaborates, for you cannot avoid it and continue to be yourself. It is, say, like mountain climbing to a mountaineer: men have tried to climb Everest, and have now succeeded, simply because (as Mallory remarked) it is *there*. This may seem a most irrational and inadequate reason to those to whom the mountains have never spoken, but to the others who know the quiet ecstasy of climbing no other answer is needed. In fact, to them any other answer seems silly.

It is hardly necessary to add that, though in worship one

comes to rest in God, this is rest in a living God. There is movement at the heart of it. One comes to rest on the bosom of an ongoing Gulf Stream. There is finality in the relationship established and yet there is always something more to expect: this is a paradox which is a simple fact to the worshiper. He speaks of "peace like a river," not of peace like a pool.

The sacramental experience and the beginnings of worship are personal. That is to say, they are not handed to us by our ancestry. They are always freshly our own. And yet we did not invent them. To the question, What impels you to worship? only one answer is ever given by the worshiper: it is God alone who calls you to Himself. He is His own muezzin. Nobody manufactured worship and persuaded the race to practice it. We do not choose to worship for this external reason or that. Religion, as Rudolph Otto says, begins with itself. Fundamentally it is not a matter of your choice or mine at all, though choice is satisfied. We are impelled to it, but gratefully. Why some do not seem to be called to it we cannot say—for the reason that the causes of worship are not in our human realm. Perhaps all are called to it but some do not recognize the call when it comes.

3. TO GOD'S INITIATIVE THE SOUL RESPONDS

The Will Is Touched

The relationship of the soul to God is that of a responder. Worship, including the individual kind which I am describing, is the *response* to the divine initiative. When you are accosted from behind the veil that separates the unseen and eternal from the visible and temporal, you do something about it, especially when you conceive God to be alive and concerned. Nowhere is the saying of the old philosophers, "Being requires action," more clearly illustrated than here: one cannot *be* in God's presence without suiting action to the circumstance. There is a temple I have visited in Madura, India, where the god is so indigenous as to be counted a kind of neighbor by the people. There the priests in midafternoon make a great beating of drums. Why? In order to wake up the god, who like any wise person in the heat of the day has been taking his siesta. Presently when they set his food before him in the sacrificial meal, they will not want to have him lose the relish of it because of drowsiness. So they rouse him. It is all quite simple and understandable. But even in this situation, as you see, although the god may be asleep for a little and then not so formidable as at other times, they do not neglect him. They respond. They worship.

Worship always reaches to the center of the human person when it is the real thing: it touches and releases the will. It concerns not a segment of the human being but a sector, not lying on the periphery but reaching to the inner part.

Undoubtedly it may have emotional accompaniments which

> Dissolve me into ecstasies
> And bring all heaven before mine eyes.

Sometimes these accompaniments—especially those which attend the immediate personal reaction to a primary sacramental experience—seem extravagant beyond reality. There is a type of psychiatrist who is likely to discredit the event which befell Saul on the road to Damascus on the ground that the seeing of a light and the hearing of a voice from the sky belong to the mentally disturbed. Undoubtedly phenomena such as these do attend highly emotional states of any kind, but who would call these the essence of the encounter between Saul and the one whom he persecuted? If you had lived in that day and had been asked whose life and thought, among all the people of the then world, would be likeliest to mold the future, I feel certain that you would never have named this obscure preacher-tentmaker who lived on the outskirts of the empire. You would have found your choice, perhaps, in the imperial house. Tiberius, then ruling, though no genius, was at least a man of prodigious application and industry who gave the whole circle of lands good laws and used his wealth to the advantage of the remotest parts of his domain. Or you might have selected Seneca the Younger, a man of about Paul's age—the counselor of emperors, an emperor himself in the realm of the arts, the masterly interpreter of the most heroic religion of the day, Stoicism. You would almost naturally have named him a candidate for future greatness. If, however, we compute greatness by the influence upon the world a man develops, the man who had the encounter on the Damascus road was the most important in the empire. Few of us can remember much about Tiberius, only a few more can quote a random line from Seneca, but the thoughts of St. Paul are the presuppositions of belief throughout Christendom. We think what we think in part because of St. Paul. Who would not be willing to see a light and hear a voice from the sky if as a result he could guide succeeding generations with strength for nineteen hundred years? The meeting, in a word, was more than its emotional accompaniments: it had its effect upon Paul's will: it determined choice, and choice determines history.

4. THE DIVINE INCURSION AND THE SOUL'S FUTURE

THE BEGINNING OF FORMAL WORSHIP

We are still in the area of Christendom in general. The events we have been describing need not have taken place within the organized Christian Church, but now we must turn to some considerations which prepare us for the fact of the church and indeed lead us to it.

Paul's encounter with deity had both an immediate and a lasting effect.

That it had an immediate effect was evident in the physical realm. Saul fell to the earth—a natural position to assume in the Orient (and perhaps everywhere else) when one feels that extremest dependence which is at the heart of worship. This is what the Bible calls "prostrating oneself"—not the token prostration of kneeling, Western style, or bowing the head, but getting down on knees and elbows. Paul showed by the very posture of his body what was going on inside of him: he was looking at God not as a philosopher might, as an object of his thought, but as a creature must, as the eternal subject. God had entered his life from beyond the limit of his own capacities and entered it radically.

At the moment, however, it is more to our purpose to note the permanent effect of the experience for Paul. When God came to Saul it was not for an afternoon call. He came to be a abiding presence. It is true that the manifestation, accompanied by the emotional eruptions I have mentioned, did not last. Other special manifestations might be expected later—notably, for Paul, those which would usher in the end of the world—but herein a *presence* of this sort differs from a *manifestation*. The latter is active, the former passive. Memory enters into this sense of presence, too—the memory of the active manifestation of a God who is forever. This is that which makes worship so exciting to the worshiper to whom God has once spoken: though God may seem passive in a subsequent time of worship, that very passivity is informed in the mind of the worshiper with the memory that He has manifested Himself actively. So the visit of Christ to Paul was forever: it was the beginning of a constant, warm, and fecund relationship. We shall take up this important matter later when we come to consider the inner nature of the church.

A sacramental experience makes subsequent, regular, formal worship possible and necessary. Once an individual has met his God, the curtain between heaven and earth is thinned to gossamer and he cannot but make plans to live in the presence of that God, returning ever and again to acknowledge Him. The basic difference between the God-man meeting in the kind of sacramental experience I have been describing and the meeting in formal worship is, as I have suggested, that the former is aureoled with the awareness that God has taken the immediate initiative, whereas in the meetings where memory plays a part, though God is present, we have a part in initiating the encounter. Worship is always a direct response to a felt experience of God or a celebration of that experience which, because God is alive, eternal, and omnipresent, becomes a re-enactment of it, though partly under our own auspices.

An initial sacramental experience sometimes, of course, comes to one during the moment of formal worship itself. So it was, apparently, in the case of Isaiah; and so, or very nearly so, in the case of John Wesley on his memorable day, May 24, 1738.

In the evening I went very willingly to a society in Aldersgate Street, where one was reading Luther's preface to the *Epistle to the Romans.* About a quarter before nine, while he was describing the change which God works in the heart through faith in Christ, I felt my heart strangely warmed.

The initial sacramental experience certainly came during formal worship to Paul Claudel. In 1886 he attended Christian mass at the Cathedral of Notre Dame in Paris. Twenty years after, the happening was still vivid in his memory:

I stood upright in the midst of the crowd near the second pillar at the entrance to the choir to the right of the vestry. And it was at that moment that the event took place that has ruled my entire life. In an instant my heart was moved, and I believed.

The techniques of most evangelistic campaigns and church missions are based upon the belief that formal worship is a likely milieu for the initial experience of God; but no one will say that the sacramental moment and ordinary worship are one and the same. The former gives content to the latter.

5. WORSHIP CONSIDERED IN ITSELF

And the Things That Accompany Worship

In every sacramental experience, whether it be the dawn encounter, sudden or gradual, through which God reveals Himself to the soul, or the formal worship which is subsequent, distinction must be made, in thought at least, between God, who is the very essence of the experience, and the sacramental vehicle through which He reveals Himself.

The extraordinary element in worship is that it is directed to God, whom the worshiper never sees or otherwise apprehends through perception by the senses. Nor can the worshiper comprehend Him. He is neither the quarry of eye, ear, or any other organ nor the result of cogitation upon anything that these alert organs bring in.

God is not an object of the senses as the things of nature are. If the inhabitants of a near-by planet succeed in launching a free-sailing sputnik which will reach the earth, and if some of them come to earth with it, there will be nothing so difficult for them to understand, if they think by a process of induction and have only what they see elsewhere in natural life to guide them, as the custom of worship to which men give themselves. They will be able to classify and appreciate men as working animals; the ants in their hills and the bees in their hives will help them understand New York and Tokyo. They will have some understanding of the interesting antics of the human courtship they will observe, for there are analogies in the lives of the lower creatures. But how will they explain the palpable fact that once a week a number of people in every community in the United States leave their homes, assemble in a building with a steeple or a tower on it, listen to a man who in their behalf will talk, or they themselves in unison will talk, with someone called God whom they themselves have never seen or heard and nobody else has ever seen or heard, and even give money to provide like curious buildings in other parts of the world in order that other people may engage in this seemingly unnatural pursuit. From this angle worship may not seem to be even sensible, for the reason that it is directed to a reality that the senses cannot apprehend.

Let us continue to stress the point, however, that though God does not come to us through the senses, it is undeniably true (as the religious man who trusts his best moments knows) that we have contact with Him. To the worshiper He is not seen or heard—but there he is. Men would not have built temples had they not been touched (to borrow a term from the realm of the senses) by a not seen and not heard something.

Nor is God a thought-out something, made available by discursive reasoning. Perhaps we should guess this from the principle of the medieval philosophers that there is nothing in the intellect which was not first in the senses—and God is not in the senses. People know God as the result of a revelation which is not subject to ordinary conceptual definition—but none the less they know Him. As Otto points out, the mystery of God does not mean the unknowableness of God: St. Paul "knows" the peace which "passeth understanding," and so does every true worshiper. God is not known in the ordinary way. Indeed, a God for whom an adequate representation in idea could be found, or who could in any way be tied to an idea, or even be proved by a series of ideas, would hardly be a God one could worship. Voltaire observed that four thousand volumes of metaphysics will not teach us what the soul is. Something similar could be said of worship, which is the meeting of one knowable mystery—the soul—with another—God. No proof of God is a substitute for God; and to one to whom God has been made known the disproof of Him is as empty as the interior of zero. Sir Arthur Eddington (joined by John Baillie) remarks that the soul and God laugh together over the idea that there is no God. Metaphysics, religious psychology, comparative religions, and all the rest of the studies that criticize and classify are marvelously useful in showing how true worship expresses itself and therefore what form true worship takes, but they are simply pensioners in the train of it: they cannot touch its essence, never quite interpret it in their own language, and therefore cannot sit in judgment upon it. True worship denounces as idols arguments of any kind that pretend to lend God support. They avail to demolish other arguments which may seem to jeopardize God's status, but this kind of battle takes place on the low plains of human intellectualization: the surge of it does not wash the heights of Olympus. Worship comes before philosophizing, which never quite overtakes it.

But now we enter into paradox in earnest; the God who is neither seen nor heard and is not susceptible of being reduced to an idea never calls a person to worship except in association with something that is seen or heard or conceptualized as an idea. Since while we live we enjoy an uninterrupted stream of consciousness made up of innumerable impressions brought in from the world outside, treasured in the foreground or the background of our mind, together with constellations of ideas derived from those impressions, it is hardly to be wondered at that worship invariably finds itself involved in perceptions of the world outside or in the reflections of them on the world inside. But the matter goes deeper.

Worship has discovered kinship with certain objects and conceptions rather than others. These remind us of God more easily than the others; they serve as vehicles for ordinary worship. Look in at a primitive society. The visitor to Polynesia will get in trouble on certain islands if he touches a sacred person or thing, enters a sacred place, or in any way interferes with a sacred ceremony, for the God that the natives have never seen or heard is in their minds inextricably tied to objects or events they do see and hear. Do not say that that idol is simply painted wood: it is painted wood *plus* for the devotee, and for him that *plus* can in no way be dissociated from the thing; to it he prays with most dreadful seriousness. Or go to an advanced civilization. Go on to India. Kailasa! Have you ever seen that? At Ellora the land rises abruptly from the plain in a great cliff, and out of that cliff has been carved, by hand, with mallet and chisel, an entire cathedral, its base level with the plain. The rock has been cut away, both externally and internally, leaving standing a seamless thing of beauty which has an integrity that its European counterparts constructed piece by piece at Chartres or Cologne cannot boast. This could hardly have sustained the devotion of its builders for the generation after generation it took to build it if it had not been for the control it exercised as a consecrated thing. God was not the thing; God was not in the thing; but here was (and is) an unbreakable God-thing relationship. In all sorts of societies it remains true that worship becomes associated with particular objects and localities. It is easier for us to worship in a church than, let us say, in a department store or at a race track. Who in fact will dispute the fact that worship of the unapprehendable God becomes linked with wholly apprehendable places, objects, or events—with anything apprehendable, in fact—even music in certain of its modes?

The uncomprehendable God has spoken through quite comprehendable ideas. Witness here the dramatic way in which Horace Bushnell came to be aware of the presence of the Most High. Writing of himself in the third person and the present tense, he confesses his astonishment in finding that he cannot

say with any emphasis of conviction that God exists. The world looks blank, and he feels that existence is getting blank also to itself . . . till, finally pacing his chamber some day, there comes up suddenly the question: "Is there then no truth that I do believe? Yes, there is one, now that I think of it: there is a distinction of right and wrong that I never doubted, and I see not how I can; I am even quite sure of it. . . ." The very suggestion seems a kind of revelation; it is even a relief to feel the conviction it brings. "Here then," he says, "I will begin. If there is a God, as I rather hope there is, and very dimly believe, he is a right God. . . ." Now the decisive moment is come. He drops on his knees and there he prays to the dim God, dimly felt, confesses the dimness for honesty's sake, and asking for help that he may begin a right life. . . . It is an awfully dark prayer, in the look of it . . . but so profoundly meant that his soul is borne up into God's help, as it were, by some unseen chariot, and permitted to see the opening of heaven even sooner than he opens his eyes.

Bushnell would have been the first to say that the series of thoughts that accompanied the incursion of the Holy Spirit in his heart was no proof of God, for God is His own master and cannot be brought to heel by any compulsion, even the compulsion of most logical thinking. I dare say that others may have had the same thoughts as Bushnell without feeling any of the quality of "revelation"—to use his word—in them. But the fact that God's presence is not ancillary to the thoughts by no means disproves the deeper fact that that presence in Bushnell's mind was associated with the thoughts.

II. Form and Essence

6. SACRAMENTS AND SYMBOLS

WORSHIP AS ATTENTION TO GOD

It has already been said that a sacramental experience makes subsequent and formal worship possible because it gives it living content. Now we are ready to connect the two kinds of religious event even more closely. If the unseen and unapprehended God never comes to us except through things which are seen or otherwise apprehended, we have these things to hand for our use when we wish to have Him repeat His coming in formal worship, that is, the worship which we ourselves have part in initiating. Used in that way the sacramental vehicle is better, I believe, called a symbol, for this word may carry the human-touch connotation which the word "sacrament" does not.

If a sacrament is what God employs to speak to us, it will be seen that none of us can control a sacrament, properly so called. It is not for us to become creators of the Creator. We cannot say the magic "This is My Body" in such a way as to compel the great God to descend from heaven and re-enact the sacrifice on Calvary—nor can any man. That his real presence may be available at communion, who will doubt, but that it is a presence compelled by the celebrant, who will affirm? Though a sacrament is a means that God uses to speak to us, it is not a means that we can use to make Him speak. The Protestant Reformation turned upon this point: the priest is not the vicegerent of God. He is God's minister.

A sacred symbol, on the other hand, may be something you and I can have a part in making. It is the sort of thing we use in formal worship, where we always try to recall a moment of sacrament. God once spoke to us through a crucifixion; you and I cannot repeat that, but if we want to converse with Him about it, it is possible for us, if we have the skill, to carve a crucifix or paint an icon which will reproduce the scene, or let our imagination play so vividly that on the canvas of our minds the crosses are set up again, the victim is nailed to the wood again, the women are hushed to trembling silence again, the soldiers curse again, and the darkness descending again takes the glint from helmet and spearhead. But this is partly of our own making: it has on it the mark of a symbol. I can throw it upon my mind as on a screen, but I cannot thereby lure the deity from paradise to give living substance to the dream. It is indeed the church's memory of an occasion when God did speak to man. It is therefore a symbol big with possibility, and there is every assurance that God will use it to speak with.

Christian symbols do not then compel God's presence. He remains free: He is God. They can be used, however, to acknowledge that He has been present in history, and in this very acknowledgment He *is* present, for once you have conceived God to be present you cannot conceive Him to be absent. He does not come and go, like created things.

The fact that the bread and wine, though they are only symbols, have so often served as the acknowledgment of God's sacramental presence is probably the reason why, by metonymy, we call the Holy Supper *the* sacrament. We all remember those blessed times when He has been much more than a conception in our worship. Whenever He has left a *result* upon us, whenever we have risen from the table with a deeper insight, a heightened vision, a firmer resolve, the symbols we have used as an acknowledgment that God has once appeared in history have been taken in hand by the Creator and Redeemer Himself and made very present sacraments.

We turn for our symbols in worship to the things, thoughts, places, in which God has already come to us. If He has used these once we cannot but associate them with His coming and pray that He will use them again. They are absolutely indispensable for worship, for they are aids to attention—and attention is the very gist of worship.

Plotinus heard God saying, "You must learn to pay attention," and this divine mandate does not seem to have changed from the third century to the twentieth. The discerning Simone Weil returns to the same truth: "Prayer consists of attention.... It is the orientation of all the attention of which the soul is capable toward God."

Now attention, as every thoughtful person knows, is a rhythmic and relating activity of the mind. It is not the ability "to look at the point of a cambric needle for one-half hour without winking." Such a feat would show a remarkable power of concentration but would not be attention. It would not produce the enlightenment which is the end of attention but would only bring about a state of hypnosis. Single-eyed attention can be sustained for only a few moments at a time and therefore keeps returning rhythmically to its object.

This means that consciousness enters into a reciprocating motion between the object of attention and other objects round about, relating them to each other. One cannot keep his attention on his hand, for instance, by holding it in front of him and simply repeating "Hand . . . hand . . . hand . . ." But attention can be maintained with relative ease as long as the hand can be seen as the center of lines of relationship with other objects over which consciousness shuttles back and forth. The hand is connected by the wrist to the arm . . . it is seen because the sun shines upon it . . . it has four fingers and a thumb . . . it can grasp the handles of things . . . it can be used for gesturing: one can keep that hand in mind without difficulty—not by attending strongly to it and it alone but by making it the central core of thought while thinking in rhythmic fashion also of other matters related to it.

This principle rules as regally on the human side of formal worship as anywhere else. Professor Hocking in a famous chapter in *The Meaning of God in Human Experience* brings out the fact that one cannot go on worshiping continuously and without change even if he should wish to do so, and that worship needs the other parts of human life, relating itself to them in long-intervaled rhythms—becoming weekly worship or daily or even hourly worship but never constant worship. But the rule of rhythmic and relating attention holds as well for the act of worship itself, narrowly considered. It is by this means that the unseen object of worship and the seen accompaniments of worship are related. At its heart the act is paying attention to God—a God whom one does not see or hear or think but toward whom one may none the less direct his mind—and the accompaniments of worship are the reflectors which carry the mind in reciprocation back to the central object.

Once the human soul has tasted the blessing of a sacramental experience it can wish for nothing so much as the continuance of the relation there established; whether God comes in judgment or in grace or both, the one hope is to maintain contact with Him. God can be depended upon: He is *there*. But how to maintain our attention in worship, that is the question; and here the accompaniments of worship which are oriented toward God and therefore constantly redirect our attention toward Him come to our aid. They are in fact the structure for formal worship.

7. ONE'S OWN AND OTHERS' SYMBOLS

THEIR CORRELATION WITH GOD'S CHARACTER

For each individual there is no accessory to formal worship more effectual than the thing or idea that gave occasion to the advent of the deity in a sacramental experience. If that bush burned with the effulgence of God's presence, I can at least go back to it with the hope that it may do so again—or, more accurately, though I am hardly likely to see it break out into flames a second time, I cannot look at it without being reminded of God's invasion of my life when it burst out the first time. The stones on which my head was lying when within it the bright ladder was set up on which the messengers from heaven to earth passed to and fro remain Beth-El for me, and I shall arrange to have the story told to all my progeny. All thoughts of the mind that accompany the sacramental moment remain helpful aids to future adoration. Otherwise Pascal would never have stitched up in his doublet the enigmatic record of that strange two hours and a half, to be discovered only at his death. There are many questions one would like to ask about the event described—especially as to what brought it on—to which there is no answer. One thing, however, is certain: to Pascal the very account of the event burned with inextinguishable meaning—

> The year of grace 1654
> Monday 23rd November, day of St. Clement . . .
> from about ten at night
> to half past twelve.
>
> FIRE
>
> God of Abraham, God of Isaac, God of Jacob,
>   Not of philosophers and savants.
> Certainty, joy, certainty, awareness, peace, joy.
>   God of *Jesus Christ* . . .

The things and ideas that are present when God, on His own as it were, breaks into the human sphere are, as is evident, many and various, yet each has its own power of reminder to the one in whose experience it is related to God's presence—for Moses the bush, for Jacob the cairn, for Pascal the strange fire in his thoughts. These will forever take them back to God.

This may well be the secret which John 10:40 contains. As a young man Jesus had come to the place on the Jordan where the picturesque and mighty John the Baptist was baptizing. He had offered himself for baptism, and in the very moment of the act he seems to have acquired the mystical knowledge that God had sent him into the world to accomplish a great purpose. But now, three years after, having found distrust and conflict mounting against him wherever he turned, he was about to face the cross itself. Was it not natural for him, in the midst of evil and in apprehension of worse evil to come, to return to the place where he first received his mission? Though we do not know what happened there, we do know that he came out of that place with strength sufficient to face any circumstance which life would throw against him. The physical and mental accompaniments of one's first encounter with God become one of the natural aids to future contact with Him.

It is important to note that the first encounter with deity is not necessarily the last, and that the association of a particular thing or thought or event with deity in the mind of any individual does not at all close that mind to associating other things or thoughts or events with God. Many and various may be the accompaniments of the divine invasion in the experience of an individual person. Browning was undoubtedly reverting to haloed moments of his own past when he wrote of

> a sunset touch,
> A fancy from a flower-bell, some one's death,
> A chorus ending from Euripides.

One has added to him, as he grows older, more than one of those memories that bless and burn, all of them pointing to the one imperial, central, unseen but seeing, unheard but hearing, God.

The possibility of a plural experience at the hands of God keeps the door of the soul open and even gives one something of hospitality to experiences other than one's own. It is natural to turn not only to the places and things, the single thoughts and clusters of thought, that marked one's own sacramental experience but also to those associated with that of others. Is it not the mark of the spiritually growing man that he comes to be constantly on the lookout in others for deeper insights into the character of the God who has come to him and to whom he is committed? Others cannot *exhibit* God, to be sure, for in order to do so it would be necessary to possess Him, which lies beyond all possibility. Even a lot of others, who call themselves the Christian Church, cannot do this. All others can do for the seeker is to show him the accompaniments of their own sacramental experiences and make him aware of the necessity they feel to respond to them adequately, in the hope that God will be pleased to repeat his revelation to the seeker through the same media and make him feel the same necessity for response. This is the meaning of *witness,* and this is the special task of the minister.

Here lies the essential difference between the minister and the teacher, though there must be something of both in every leader of the church. A teacher tells of things, persons, relationships, and events, but a minister tells how God has used things, persons, relationships, and events to reveal His presence. In this the minister can never bring God into the realm of objects which can be taught, never teach Him as one can teach chemistry; he cannot produce God for the benefit of the congregation, cannot put a few drops of something or other into a test tube, warm it, and create God for the edification of beholders. He is sometimes in an impossible position, for it is just *that* which some people think he is paid to do, and *that* is strictly what he cannot do. He can simply tell the story of revelation by pointing to the accompaniments and results of it. He can witness by using these means as evidences. All he can handle and manipulate are these evidences—not the God to whom he believes they point. That in itself should give him the humility which is the first requisite of a good minister.

But to go back to our seeker, as he looks out upon what might be called the religious world, that is, the world of things and ideas that people associate with God. What a vast profusion he sees! Burning bushes, temples in the year that King Uzziah died, roads to Damascus (to say nothing of Seventh Symphonies, Masses in B Minor), as well as cosmological, ontological, teleological, and other philosophical plays of thought. Who can count the circumstances that have attended the awareness of God in the minds of men?

These accompaniments of theophany have been grouped together in the great religions of the world, not to say the denominations within the several religions. The difference between faiths is a subject altogether too vast, and for our purposes too irrelevant, to be considered here, but I am glad to note that it is again coming to the fore in institutions of higher learning. I have come to believe that the divinity schools of the broadgauged Protestant type must do what they can to give their students a chance to understand as best they may the great non-Christian religions of the world. The effect of this encounter is never a superficial syncretism or a jerry-built eclecticism, which are usually the products of enthusiastic ignorance. It is only through the spectacles of abstraction that one sees all religions as essentially the same with only surface differences. It is truer to say with Dr. Latourette that they are essentially different with surface resemblances. They are alike, to be sure, in that God, the one God, tries to speak through them all, but they are quite different in their apprehension of what He is trying to say to the race. I have never found the reading of devotional literature from areas outside of Christendom diluting to my Christian faith. Some ideas from outside have to be dismissed, some may be incorporated in our faith—but this is not incorporating a non-Christian faith. It is simply amplifying the stock of thoughts which are illuminated by Christ's revelation, just as Stoicism and the mystery religions were illuminated by it in the early centuries. Non-Christians may have some hesitation about studying the Christian faith, but it is high time for Christian schools, relying on the ultimateness of Christ, to become as lovingly understanding of other people as they possibly can. It is good to note that the International Missionary Council is setting up centers in various parts of the world for just this purpose.

I mention the world religions now just to note that there is a relation between their several insights into the character of God and the form of sacramental vehicle through which the insights have come and of the subsequent symbols used. This is a matter of consummate importance.

One could hardly have stood on the outskirts of the crowd at the time of sacrifice to the god Moloch, for instance, without having some idea of the kind of god his worshipers thought him to be. Those horrible flames must have hinted that the god who had originally made himself felt through them, and for whom they were now a continuing reminder, was destructive and terrible.

Again, if Allah is in complete abstraction from the ways of earth, how could I speak to him better, or better imagine him speaking to me, than through the geometrical figures of the mosque, which are not the likeness of anything that is in heaven above, or in the earth beneath, or in the water under the earth? There is correspondence between the accompaniments of worship and the object of the worship as the worshiper understands that object.

The very posture and gestures of the worshiper have a relation to the character of the God worshiped as it is apprehended by the worshiper. The crown of the life of a Buddhist is said to be that moment of transport when, bathed in silence, he holds in his mind the thought of formlessness and loses his identity in the Timelessly Real. The man who will prepare himself for the coming of this god who underlies all things and in whom is no individuality at all (if it be right to call him a god) will be in meditation, rapt from the world. So the figure of the Buddha, as an aid to worship, is shown seated or reclining in quiet, always immersed in thought. I am told that nothing astonishes a Buddhist more than a first view of a crucifix. He is amazed that anyone could regard as a religious symbol the representation of a man not sunk back into himself but facing the world, feeling the world at its worst. How can this conduce to worship? Obviously it cannot conduce to worship of the Buddhist type, because there is no correlation between that object and the ultimate object of Buddhist adoration. A symbol by its very definition suggests some correspondence with that which is symbolized.

Many have pressed into duty this idea of correspondence in considering the two great parts of Christianity, Catholicism and Protestantism, pointing out as well as they may that the accompaniments and supports of the Catholic faith are likely to be such as can be perceived by the senses, while the Protestant faith has an inveterate tendency to look into thought for its witnesses. So the Catholic mass is centered in something all can see, whereas the Protestant sermon is, or should be, something all can think. How magnificent are the architecture, sculpture, liturgy, and other aids to worship preserved in the Catholic Church, and what extraordinary range and versatility Protestant theology has achieved, especially in the realm of Biblical criticism! That any religion could have done with its sacred book what Protestantism has done with the Bible, reaching a point where there is a meeting of thoroughgoing criticism and deeply held belief, is one of the world's wonders. But I must not say more about this here, for at the moment we are concerned only with noting that the alleged difference in the Catholic and the Protestant types of symbol, the one material, the other conceptual, must mean a difference in the conceptions of God held by the two. We should guess that Catholicism saw God more as a Creator, Maker, Artist, while Protestantism looked at Him rather as a Thinker, the Guardian and Imparter of the Truth; but if this distinction was ever true, it is surely fading into irrelevance today, when the more sensitive on both sides are becoming aware of and repairing their deficiencies so that it would be utterly foolish to say that Catholicism is prepared to sacrifice truth or Protestantism beauty. Each is picking up the needed symbolizations to fill out their common insight into the character of the God and Father of our Lord.

Both types of symbol—the material and the intellectual—are useful. Say rather that they are indispensable. When a person grows up in a church overlaid with a plethora of liturgical details, there is need of intellectual guideposts. Historians have told me that in the Europe of the sixteenth century it was the churches which were accustomed to preaching wherein was found the courage to make reformation early. There are churches which are strait-jacketed by credal details: here the breath of liturgical beauty will give refreshment to many a drooping soul. I like the look of what might be called contemporary Puritanism, which finds beauty in straight thinking and straight thinking in beauty, with both issuing in action.

In the midst of all it must be remembered that symbols which are mere embellishments are always superfluous and really evil. There is a deep craving for simplicity among the sensitive. Bishop Hall spoke of the remarkably small number of tenets that a Christian needs. Correspondingly, the things it takes to make worship are relatively few. Perhaps we may say that there is a correlation between the simplicity which is in God's love and the simplicity which should be sought in all true worship.

If we carry in our minds the fundamental notion of the necessary correlation between the character of the symbol and that of the object of devotion which is symbolized, we shall be helped to a better understanding of the meaning of the Christian Church.

8. THE CHRISTIAN CHURCH

Ecclesia Ecclesiata

If your experience was like mine, it was only some time after you entered the Christian Church that you became a Christian. You were born in a Christian family of which the church was a part of the cultural life. You believed in God, no doubt; you had never had occasion to disbelieve in Him; and it was wholly natural that when you achieved the age considered appropriate for the act by your parents, you were confirmed in the church. If I were to do it over again, I doubt if I should have it otherwise, for the church helped me to understand myself in the light of the experiences of thousands upon thousands of others like myself, who had been touched by God's Spirit and were looking for further leading.

To Saul, blinded by more than the sun on the Damascus Road, the experience of Christ came first, the church later, but for most of us the order is reversed. The institution beckons toward the experience, and this it is fitted to do as the total complex of those accompaniments of worship we have been considering, those symbols, material and intellectual, which can catch the eye. To borrow a manner of phrase-making from Spinoza, we might call this the *ecclesia ecclesiata*—the church seen in its results, the church as a historical deposit, the church we can handle and consider, as we handle and consider other things, the perceptible church in the perceptible world.

One brought up in Christendom can hardly say that he encounters the Christian Church only *after* the Holy Spirit (in what I have been calling the sacramental experience) has moved him to realize that he lives not only in a worldly but also in another realm, for the thousand and one impressions he has directly or indirectly gained from the church before that moment will have provided the form for that experience itself. It is doubtful, for instance, if Bushnell would even have thought of awaiting God at the point of his dedication to goodness if it had not been for his own earlier Christian nurture. In this sense most of us could add an *ecclesiaque* as well as a *filioque* to our creed, for we must admit that the Holy Spirit has proceeded to us through the church (as well as through the Son). God has used the church as an auxiliary in His disclosure of Himself. Yet it would be as erroneous to insist that God first speaks to everybody through the direct or indirect medium of the church, as it is surely a dogmatic denial of human experience to hold that the Holy Spirit has spoken only where Christ has been preached. That he speaks in fullness only where Christ has come, what Christian would deny? But there may be throughout God's world a preparation for the Gospel which fits those who erect altars to the unknown God for the preaching of the St. Pauls.

Actually it makes no difference whether God used the church to disturb your spirit into thinking of Him or not. If under any circumstances whatever you have felt His sacramental touch, you will receive aid and comfort from settling down amidst the forms of the *ecclesia ecclesiata,* for they are the witnesses of the centuries to the same kind of experience that you have had. They must indeed mean little to you if you come to the church wholly without the sacramental preparation. One can hardly appreciate the glory and tragedy of *Romeo and Juliet* until he has himself been in love. (One can discern little meaning in the prayers, hymns, and other aids to worship in the church until he has found himself standing in the need of prayer or longing to sing praise to the God who has found him.)

(The minister of the church must know that he is serving at least two kinds of people in the parish. There are those who have sought and found: they still continue their further search into the richness of the life which is hid with Christ in God, but their faith has brought them that serenity and strength which make them the living nucleus of the congregation. At the other extreme are those whom the Spirit has touched into inquiry but who have not yet come upon any answer to which they can yield their full and satisfied assent.) In the pews of many a church in New England sit those over whose heads are discernible (in the eye of fancy) not haloes but question marks. It is these of whom I am thinking at the moment.

The church cannot bring God out before them in such a way that they are compelled to believe, and it would not do so even if it could. But the church can lay before them the accompaniments that have led others to believe. The church is a vast place of witness, and by a man like Horace Bushnell, the chrism of new life pouring over his soul, and by men who have not received so secure an answer, the church can be recognized as the society of those to whom the Spirit has spoken in one way or another. However far or not far their new life has gone, it can be lived out and amplified in the church. And this, I think, is what we may point out to our young people who have been moved by a divine spirit to ask the meaning of human life: they may be bored by the sermons they hear, they may be offended in the music of a too amateur choir, they may not like the people who occupy the high pews, but for all this the church affords them their best chance to sustain their rhythmic attention upon their basic problem and its answer, for they will find others doing the same thing. The people of the Bible are doing this: the Bible in its wholeness will preach them a sermon more eloquent than any they will hear from the pulpit, and in the church will be found, if they will look for them, witnesses which will be a most momentous aid to lend historical and social relevance to their own Christian inquiry and response. Horace Bushnell and the others whose space-time lives have been penetrated from the heavenly side find the church pointing to the same God who has waylaid them personally, and to the church they presently add their own religious histories in such a way that the memories of the Yale rooms themselves become part of the equipment of the church to remind the entire membership of the imminent (I do not mean immanent: I mean threatening) fact of God in the world. The church becomes the treasure house of all these memories; and as the gleam of the Nibelungen hoard in the cave attracted men's minds to avarice, so the light from this ensemble of experiences calls men's thoughts to divinity.

I am awed by the vastness of witness which even the smallest church affords. I pick up a mimeographed calendar in a rural church and find there in the order of service a prelude from Gounod's *Gallia,* which is an intercessory prayer lifted to God by a religious man for his country; a hymn by Washington Gladden written under the shared burden of the needs of individual members of his parish; a prayer from the 1552 Book of Common Prayer, which breathes the hopes of the most consecrated men in England that the churches would not fall apart into warring sects, as they actually did; the Scripture lessons, which carry the congregation back into the dawns and darknesses that animated men and women like ourselves centuries upon centuries ago; to say nothing of the sermon and the other parts which were also transcripts from life. If you want to get acquainted with the human race on the edge where it is invaded from the Godward side, where can you go with more profit than to the church on the corner, or on the common? All I can say for myself is that my own feeble flame has been again and again enhanced from the various fires that collected together burn on the altar of the church. It is through the sacramental accompaniments of the insights of others, kept by the church as symbols, that one may go through the same experiences himself.

In theory, the church is no less drawn to the man than the man to the church, for each has something of insight to give the other. In actuality, however, one might as well say that when I release a ball from my hand the earth bounces up to it as it bounces down upon the earth. It is true that each is a body that exerts gravitational force on the other, but there, after all, the similarity ceases. The shaft of light that has fallen from heaven on the man's mind is hardly to be compared to the opulence of sunshine that has been shed upon the broad landscape of the church. The skilled minister is one who by preaching and in conversation is able to help John Jones and Mary Smith and the innumerable others in his parish, who in one way or another have had some intimation of God's interest in them, to see that the church is the place in which these intimations can be sustained and given depth by the process of sharing in witness.

An interesting thing about the Christian Church is that while you are searching for it you find that it is searching for you. Here it seems to be connected in a direct line of descent from the Hebrew prophets through whom God created the Hebrew people and through them the people of the New Covenant. God's word to them was always social in its outreach—"Go and tell this people . . ."—and its outreach had two concentric applications. The prophets were sent to the house of Israel, for these were the people chosen to do a great work. Israel was the target of the line I have quoted. But in an important sense the prophets were also sent to the world: "Thou shalt go to all that I shall send thee," "All the nations of the earth shall be blessed" in Abraham. A Hebrew could feel that God had dignified him by making him a member of a chosen people, but that that people was chosen only to be a blessing to the world. The same relationships apply to the Christian Church, except that the mark of membership in it is not blood but belief. That it exists to bless the world is one of its axioms: it seeks all that are lost—or not yet found.

\So far as I know there is no other religion in the world except Christianity in which the human response to deity becomes a worshiping *church.*\In a certain sociological sense each religion is related to its culture, which in turn is the coefficient of a society, but among non-Christian peoples, so far as I know them, their religion seems far less to be actually creative of a clean-cut society than is Christianity. I suppose we may say that there have been only two other missionary religions—Buddhism and Islam—a fact which in itself would seem to indicate that the society-creating religions are few. Furthermore, neither of these non-Christian types have found *love* so pronouncedly in God's disclosure of Himself as to produce a church as Christians know it. There is surely a difference between a Buddhism which stimulates research into one's deepest self and a Christianity which, without disparaging such research, regards it as a means for the enrichment of spiritual conversation in community. Mohammedan worship in a mosque of a Friday morning may appear to have some kinship with the congregational worship of Christians of a Sunday morning, but the resemblance is of course only superficial. When congregations were banned in Turkey under Mustafa Kemal Pasha, worship

in the mosque went unmolested because everybody knew that
the rite there merely brought together a number of persons to
perform their own individual orisons with the help of the
leader in front. It was only the dervishes that were exiled, for
theirs were undoubtedly group meetings—but their worship is
rather more hypnotic than social. Only Christianity, I think,
has positively required a church as a witness to its belief in a
God of love.

One of the reasons why an individual whom God has touched
finds the church so grateful a place to be is that it can make a
witness to God which he cannot. He cannot be a society by
himself, but the church can be and is a society of love witness-
ing to God's society-creating grace.

As a member of the church an individual not only can but
must contribute to strengthening it as the church. A man who
has already entered into communion with God in a private
sort of way feels that something has been added to his experience when he is placed in a community where he cannot be
content to pray only, "*My* father, who art in heaven. . . ." God
is his father, to be sure, but now he knows that God cannot be
his father without also being father to the rest of mankind, and
in a special, self-conscious way to the rest of the church. He cannot say "Our Father" in sincerity without feeling the need of
someone to say it with. When conscience asks, "What do you
mean by *our*," and he responds, "Mine and my brother's," conscience immediately returns, "Then go and find your brother
and bring him to worship with you." This is the witness of the
church, felt by all its members.

(The man in search of others to whom God has spoken finds
the church searching for him. The church cannot be the church
in its fullness without *all*.)

9. CHRIST AT THE CENTER

Ecclesia Ecclesians

So the man who has begun to ask questions about God and even begun to find a provisional answer is brought into the church, where others have begun to ask questions about God and where the answer has many times been found. This is the church that one can see with the eye or apprehend with the mind—the *ecclesia ecclesiata*. And now if his mind be active he will not be content to rest thus in the porch of the temple: he must "go in to the god" as the Greeks used to say. He is within the circumference, but he knows that a circumference must have a center. If the church is one, it must have one source. He has a story to tell about his encounter with God, and so has the man next to him. So indeed have others they meet there, like St. Augustine and the Augustinian monk Martin Luther. What holds them all together?

Is there one word, is there one figure, is there one sacramental point in the life of the church which throws light on all the other such points? If there is one reason for the church, what is it?

At this point the seeker comes upon what Father Tyrrell called that strange man on the cross.

It is Jesus Christ that gives the church power to walk.

The life of Jesus is in part a *memory* in the church, and what a memory it is! The story of his life and death in an obscure end of the Roman Empire has been told and retold, I suppose, more often than the story of any other single man. It is still a subject big with inspiration for artists in every medium. No other folk song which has emerged from the pathos of Negro America carries the ineffable blend of sweetness and agony which is brought to the listening soul in "I was there when they crucified my Lord." The crucified Christ at the beginning and continuing at the heart of the church is the great central fact which gathers together and enhances the meaning of all the experiences of God which the people of the church have known. It is testimony to his centrality that when he is lifted up he draws to him so many men who, in a myriad of different circumstances, have had the dimness of their soul lighted by light from above. When one has been wrought upon by the Most High so that his soul pants for Him as the hart pants for the water brooks, he will find the church, and at its heart the figure of Christ, to be the best of all mirrors to reflect attention upon the Lord God Himself. This even a historical memory can do.

But when the church speaks of its living Christ, it refers to something more than a memory. A memory in itself is not quite alive. Communion with a memory is not the equal of personal contact. It may be dear, but so are remembered kisses after death, as Tennyson tragically recalls. A memory is to the reality as the wraith of Odysseus' mother was to the real Anticlea, unsubstantial, fading, and blown by the wind. St. Paul could not have said with full meaning, "I can do all things through the memory of a Christ who has died." That would hardly have strengthened him. And what but darkness would there have been in the cry "Not I, but the memory of one who is gone, liveth within me."

In any case, Christ provides a most peculiar kind of historical memory. This is the memory of a God who acts in history, who is forever alive. As we have pointed out in another connection, it is the *past memory of a present God*. But the living Christ is more than this: he is more than the memory of someone dead who reminds of a God who is alive.

The living Christ is the *past memory of a present God who keeps His Christ alive,* or in reality and less roundaboutly, *a presence in himself.* There is no having a living Christ and a dead God, or a living God and a dead Christ. The two go together—and the church does not believe that the Jesus of Nazareth, who lived a life of love, died a death of love, and so revealed a God of love, is *dead.* This the God of love whom he revealed does not permit. When it is said that Jesus is alive, it is not meant that he is available to sense perception, even partially. He is not a spook. He does not belong to the land of faery. Those who stay out of the church because of misunderstanding at this point should have the reassurance that Christians regard beliefs of this sort as superstitious. Christ is alive as God is alive, God having taken him to Himself. The best way to describe him is by the word already used, a *presence.*

This presence of the living Christ, which would be nothing if it were not for his historical, and rather less if it were not for his timeless, dimension, becomes then the best mediator between God and man. Obviously he is not the only vehicle of mediation between God and man, for God has made man aware of Himself through many a vehicle, but he can be called *the* Mediator because he is the best. He is at once concrete and eternal. No burning bush was ever more concrete than he, for what is more dreadfully so than a man crucified? "It is the invisibility of religion that destroys us," said the martyr Dietrich Bonhoeffer—and Christ protects against that. Yet no categorical imperative, no distinction between right and wrong, such as proved the divine way for Bushnell, is more present, persistent, and inevitable. He is as eternal as the moral code. He is simply the best means God can use for making His character known. Jesus of Nazareth is with us on the side of history, seen and heard, but we meet him also on the side of the not seen and not heard, where God lives. He is a mediator whose presence lends meaning to our memory of him, and whose memory gives distinctiveness to his presence. The almost forgotten but now reviving stanza of Watts's "When I survey . . ." brings out this duality-in-unity clearly enough:

> His dying crimson like a robe
> Spreads o'er his body on the tree;
> Then am I dead to all the globe,
> And all the globe is dead to me.

Nothing is surer than that *dying* and *crimson* and *robe, body* and *tree* belong to this world, but how could the poet have made it more certain that the relationship to Christ is actually not of this world than by averring that in Christ's presence the globe and he were dead to each other?

To speak with the nicest accuracy I can summon, I identify the living Christ as Jesus of Nazareth. This is a judgment regarding historical facts. Either he lived in Palestine nineteen hundred years ago or he did not. I think he did, but no absolute answers are available in this realm. I think he did because of the church's memory of him. The best way to account for that memory is to accept as a fact the substance of the story of his life. And part of the church's memory of him is that he stepped from history into eternity in such a way as to make himself available in both realms. This is what the resurrection appearances mean. The early church's faith in a loving God did not derive from some general idea, some Kantian category, but from the awareness that a particular person, who had given himself in total love for his fellows, had been raised from the dead. It was a paradoxical idea, but it set the course for Christian thought at its fundamental level. From the point of view of historical common sense, reasoning from effect to cause, and given the fact that the church today believes in a living Christ with a historical past, the origin of that church by and large was probably as the church has thought it to be.

But suppose I am wrong in my historical judgment. Is my whole awareness of a living Christ thereby proved a hallucination? I should hardly say so. The resurrection of a man does not necessarily bring me closer to God. Resurrections might become frequent: I should not thereby know God as a God of love. But the interesting thing about the crucifixion and resurrection of Christ is that God himself is, as it were, stained with the blood and illumined with the light of them. After you have seen Christ, you cannot think of God otherwise than as a God of love. This is the crowning illustration of the correspondence that exists between the sacramental medium, which in this case is Christ, and the deity which that medium displays. If the ancient Greek, after seeing the statue by Phidias at Olympia, could never imagine Zeus in any other form, how transcendently true it is for the Christian worshiper that the live memory of Christ and the fact of God for which it constantly claims attention become so closely identified that the one almost becomes the other. I cannot look toward God without seeing Christ: He is in Christ, taking away the sins of the world. Suppose then, for the sake of argument, that I am wrong in my historical judgment that Christ lived and died and rose again: I am not wrong about God's looking at you and me through the eyes of someone exactly like the Christ of the Bible stories. The presence of that kind of God I cannot deny: it has all the absoluteness of that which compels belief, and I may legitimately call Him the living Christ. I clothe this indisputable presence, which is God infused with the church's memory of Jesus, with my own historical judgment that this is veritably Jesus of Nazareth risen from the dead, as the creed says. I may be wrong in my historical interpretation of the origin of this presence but I am not wrong in my awareness of the presence. Of that one may have the same kind of certainty that he has of his own presence.

The essence of the Christian experience at the Holy Table is the living Christ. Since God was and is in him, since in him God did and does invade human history, he is the sacramental vehicle of God's coming. In a true sense, he is the real sacrament, as the ceremonial rite which we often call the sacrament is not. The bread and wine and the words and thoughts that go with them are symbols that we ourselves have a part in supplying, but his presence, which alone gives meaning to these symbols, is the pure gift of God. And he is a strange kind of sacrament: he is a sacrament alive. His is a life-giving presence. Through him God saves us to a kind of life worth being saved for. His loving presence, although, and indeed in part because, it is a relentlessly judging presence, is the best of all sacraments. He becomes the center for all who have had sacramental experience: he is the answer to every question instigated by the Holy Spirit.

To discover the living Christ in the church is to take one's place in the *ecclesia ecclesians,* the church at its creative point, the church coming into history with its message and demonstration of renewal, the church not dead but living, not a cluster of symbols (important as they are in their place) but itself the continuation of God's sacramental incursion into the needy human scene.

At least for a person brought up in Christendom, whose early insights are likely to take a form not uninfluenced by the church, the symbols of the church, that is, the physical things and ideas it associates with God's revelation, do not deny the fact of the sacramental experience that has come to him. He has a witness to make which is not repugnant to that made by the church. He takes the church's witness seriously, looks in the direction it points, and presently has, in effect, a new and deeper sacramental experience in respect of Christ. Undoubtedly there are those who are led by the Holy Spirit immediately to Christ, as St. Paul was, but I rather think there are more who, like Bushnell, find the first rays of divine light shining on their souls through some other not discordant experience which has provisional status. It is the same Holy Spirit which affords the inner testimony to each; and once God speaks to a man through Christ, though He may have whispered to him through others, the man feels himself a full member of the *ecclesia ecclesians*. He now no longer lives among the symbols alone: he too has had the experience which the symbols of the church commemorate. He has found that he can respond to God more fully in the church than out of it and now he has discovered what makes the church the church.

III.   Various Dimensions

10. WORSHIP: THE END THAT CROWNS ALL

Its Primordial and Eschatological Quality

The best place to come to understand the effect of Christ upon the church is in the church's corporate worship.

We have already called attention to the fact that Christianity (with Christ as its center) alone among the religions of the world calls a church into being; and it follows that congregations of Christ's church, met for worship, are different from any other gatherings of the kind. Those crowds at the Shinto shrine at Ise are not like a Christian congregation; nor are the company of Zen monks sitting back to back at the monastery in Kyoto; nor the people gathered at the little shrine at the head of the village green in the Marathi country nor the tens of thousands at the great shrine in Madura; nor the dancers in the temple court in Tibet nor those in the Shoshone reservation in our own West. The Christian gathering for worship is different from the rest because Christ is different.

Too often, even in the Christian congregation, the spirit that rules is simply the spirit of the community. The church unfortunately cannot protect itself against the insinuation of a mere group spirit, be it a town spirit, a class spirit, or even a national spirit, into its symbols. Christ is displaced by a sometimes quite respectable tribal god. There is a cathedral in the Middle East whose walls are so covered with plaques commemorating the heroism of British army members in that part of the world that it is easier to think of it as an outpost of empire than as a throne room of the king of all kings. Kipling speaking to his fellow Englishmen called Westminster Abbey "the abbey that makes us say, 'We.'" There is something fine about that, but there is something dangerous about it, too, if and when such a place as Westminster ceases to be the abbey that makes us say, "Thou." Some of our own churches in the southland read segregationist ethics into the mind of Christ, as we in the northland undoubtedly read our own culture. There is no protection against this common failing except the regular, conscious, and complete rededication of ourselves to him as a living presence.

But when Christ rules, then the church becomes its creative self and all relationships fall into the place for which God has destined them. Consider those relationships at the moment of true worship in his presence.

Christ is clearly the means through which the *vertical* relationship between God and man is best maintained. You cannot take him seriously and believe that God has cut Himself off from man or could be content to do so. The God who has used Christ as His sacramental vehicle is not one who lives alone in heaven—not Aristotle's God, who lives in such perfection that He can think only perfect thoughts and therefore, since He alone is perfect, thinks only about Himself. He is not the apotheosis of the magnanimous man of the Eudemian ethics, for though like that man, great of soul and faculty, disdainful of what is contrary to reason, pained if denied due esteem, virtuous in ways which can be practiced in a seventh heaven, He has what the magnanimous man has not: love. For love's sake He has invaded human life: for love's sake He stands at the door of every human heart and knocks. This is made plain in Christ.

And with love goes creativity. Forgiveness itself is a moral cleaning of the slate in preparation for a new creation. It is the declaration of the chance to begin again. But the whole mood of that worship which is electric with Christ's presence is that of man on the edge of discovery. The Redeemer brings us to meet the Creator. The scientist working and dreaming his way into a new conception of nature, the artist poised before he captures and transmits to canvas a contour he sees only dimly in his mind, and the saint asking Christ how he can be used in the redemption of the world are all potential artificers of the future. The saint may differ from the others in that he gives glory where glory is due—though many a scientist and artist does the same. All I am emphasizing at the moment is that in worship in Christ's presence the line from God to man carries upon it love and creativity.

Worship in Christ's presence also exhibits and creates the kind of relationship which is called for in men toward God—that of grateful and definite dedication. An act of will is required. If God has no character, no individuality, as it were, then obviously you cannot dedicate yourself definitely to Him. Perhaps you may do it indefinitely, but I think there is really no such thing as indefinite dedication. The God who en-Christed Himself provides brunt for decision: you can be either for or against Him. He is not a Brahma who can say

> Far or forgot to me is near;
>> Shadow and sunlight are the same;
> The vanished gods to me appear;
>> And one to me are shame and fame—

or as Andrew Lang puts it, parodying Emerson:

> I am the batsman and the bat,
>> I am the bowler and the ball,
> The umpire, the pavilion cat,
>> The roller, pitch, and stumps, and all.

You can decide neither for nor against this kind of God, but for or against Christ you must decide. In Christ is preserved individuality as an essence of the eternal God. He is as individual as a lover, and must be loved as an individual, not as a generality, not as something so deeply suffused in all things that no decision can be made about it. Christians, thanks to Christ, love God: they do not become merged in Him in a way which liquifies the will.

[The *horizontal* relationship between man and man which Christ in worship evokes is equally noteworthy. It is a matter of enormous moment, as we have already pointed out, that a society comes into being in response to Christ. The door into his throne room is a curious one: no man walking selfishly alone may enter it, but two men or more, helping each other, can find easy entrance. We cannot follow Christ himself without stumbling into the innumerable recipients of his grace, the man born blind, the lepers, Mary, and all mankind, indeed. The God whom he reveals draws forth from us a love which is more than love for God alone. This love loves what its love loves. It focuses upon God, but since the love of God is upon His children, the love of the worshiper goes out to them, including all his fellow worshipers and beyond them the whole family of man. "Beloved, let us love one another: for love is of God. He that loveth not knoweth not God. If a man say, I love God, and hateth his brother, he is a liar. This commandment have we from him, that he who loveth God love his brother also." There is, to be sure, an individual response to the mystical presence of deity, but when one hides this in a napkin and fails to make it socially available, the response lacks something of Christian completeness. It is just here that the apprehension of God that comes through Christ proves ampler than that which comes through other sacramental channels. Sometimes one hears it said that all worship, including what appears to be corporate, is really individual; of Christian worship it is truer to say that it is always corporate, even when it appears to be individual, for there is no such thing as an acceptance of God's fatherhood through Christ unaccompanied by an acceptance of man's brotherhood. The Christian worshiper will join with all others who will join with him in glorifying God, and all together will dedicate themselves to the well-being of their brother men. Though this worshiper may seem to ordinary eyes to come into the church service quite alone, he actually takes the hand spiritually of all the other members of the church and leads to the throne of grace all the needy people of the world. It is not strange that the idea of the church—its members the redeemed, who have heard God's voice, its doors open to all humanity— dominates so much of Christian thought: it is hard to see how the God and father of our Lord Jesus Christ could be responded to in any other way.)

In corporate worship in Christ's presence three ultimate entities are discovered—God and the worshiper and the worshiper's brother man—and the relations between them are eternal. (*The relation of God to the worshiper is one of forgiving and creative love; that of the worshiper to God one of loving dependence and dedication; and that of the worshiper to his fellow man one of loving witness to God's will.*) These relationships, however variously they may be expressed, are ultimate. In our worship, to use Pindar's great phrase, we become what we are.

Perhaps I should more modestly say that these are the changeless essences I find in corporate worship. You may find others, though I dare say there will be similarities. At any rate, the moment of worship is, I believe, a better time to find those essences than any other, for then the soul throws off the outer world's controls, bares itself with all its conscious and subconscious contents, all its present and its past, to the God of all mankind. Only perfect trust, in face of perfect love and infinite forgiveness, can do this; but when it is done, all perspectives are washed clean.

This is undoubtedly the reason why worship in Christ's presence may be as refreshing as the morning. The soul has the sense of being at the dawn of things. Here are the fundamental entities and the primordial relationships. All of human possibility lies ahead. The present intricacies of human society which have developed in the sinuous course of history are done away, and the contacts are simple. Love has its way and is crowned with hope. The throb of life in any form is wonderful but here we are in the very matrix of life itself. The Creator's finger is upon his created ones and they are ready to respond.

The act of Christian worship has an eschatological quality to it. At the end of the world, when time has run its course, if life has any meaning, God will remain and you and I will not have ceased to be ourselves, for only He and we through our connections with each other are the bearers of meaning. In what state you and I shall then be found I do not know except that our relation to God will be precisely what it is now—and our relation to each other, the intercessory relation in which we lay our mutual needs before God in love, will be the same as that of worshipers. In worship we apprehend eternal relationships which the passage of the years, the centuries, the aeons, will not alter. "That old common arbitrator, time," will *not* one day end them. Here avails the saying of R. W. Dale of Birmingham, better known in Britain perhaps than in America.

To be at a church meeting, apart from any prayer that is offered, any hymn that is sung, any words that are spoken, is for me one of the chief means of grace. To know that I am surrounded by men and women who dwell in God, who have received the Holy Ghost, with whom I am to share the eternal righteousness and eternal rapture of the great life to come, this is blessedness. I breathe a divine air.

When we gather with our neighbors of a Sunday morning for worship we are not far from the kingdom of heaven. When we pray that God's will may be done on earth as it is in heaven, the prayer already begins to be answered in the relationships of corporate worship. This is a consideration to transfigure the routine of church life and lend zest to all our living.

Of course I do not mean that eternity is only an extension of time. Not at all. I mean that the essences and relationships discoverable in corporate worship have in them something which, being timeless, can persist beyond time, however we may be clothed with newness of form in God's tomorrow.

If one asks, How do you know all this? How can you detect eternal relationships in time? the simplest reply is that these things are known as one knows God. There is a self-authenticating quality in worship (and how could it be otherwise if it is an end in itself?) which delivers it from dependence upon ordinary argument. To find out about it, therefore, I do not go to scientists or philosophers as such, in spite of the deep esteem one must have for them in their own field. Most certainly I do not go to the skeptic, whose feet are firmly planted on his particular type of dogmatism, the absolute certainty that he never can be certain. Surely I shall not go to the man who has never honestly undertaken to worship, as one does not go to gypsies to learn the principles of architecture. To discover what worship is it seems natural to go to those who worship; and from them, who are sensitive to the deeper and subtler claims of life at this point, we learn that part of the consciousness of the worshiper, in the Christian area at least, is the sense of the soul standing in a relation to God and to other souls which is simply timeless.

To accept this fact is to lay hold of the ends which should be striven for in all worship and to acquire a norm of basic relationships for church life as a whole. One may indeed say that the entire task of the church simply stated is to extend into the totality of life the relationships already present in common worship. It is for us therefore to try to understand what these relations are.

The thesis of these lectures is that in our Christian experience of common worship there are discoverable the eternal relationships which exist between God and man, and man and man, and that it therefore behooves us to recognize what these relationships are, to emphasize them more surely in our worship, and to apply them in every part of the church's life.

Water, whether it be found at the equator or at one of the poles, whether on the peak of Everest or the bottom of the Philippines Trench, or for that matter on Jupiter or Betelgeuse, is always basically the same, two atoms of hydrogen being fixed in an unchanging relation to one of oxygen. If there is any disturbance in this relationship it ceases to be water. In some such way it may be said that the relationships within every part of the church are relatively simple and that if they are altered the church ceases to be itself.

And the point at which these relationships are most clearly distinguishable is the moment in which soul is related to soul and all to God in corporate worship.

11. THE MINISTER OF CHRIST

THE BEARER OF THE DIVINE-HUMAN CONVERSATION

Let us recapitulate. We have spoken of God's initiating the meeting between Himself and any man through His Holy

Spirit. We have pointed out that in formal worship, in which a man seeks to repeat this meeting, he turns toward those things which God has associated with His revelation of Himself and which therefore help him to pay God due attention. And we have indicated that a man finding his way into the Christian Church, on discovering that his own insights are in every way greatened by the church's, is likely to make those of the church his own—the crown of them being the apprehension of the historical and living Christ.

We have also enumerated the relationships which are cardinal to the life of worship. What now is the place of the minister of Jesus Christ in his church? Plainly his task is to help make these relationships prevail—to witness to God's love for man, to lead men in love to God, and to help them to look in love upon one another, all under the cross of the living Christ. When these matters are attended to, the church is itself.

Here we must hark back again to the truth that Christianity is a religion of meeting. God meets with man, man with God, and man with man. Only personal beings can meet in love, only eternal beings can meet in eternal love, and in God's grace a meeting which casts its reflection on the screen of eternity takes place in corporate worship in the church. This is a meeting, not an absorption. None of these entities are reduced to negation in a gelatinous mysticism. Even in Buddhism, according at least to some of its masters, individuality is not lost in *nirvana*. Whether or not this is true, it is certain that the faith of the church emphasizes the element of meeting in worship and, as its last view of human life, sees not an ocean of consciousness in which all drops are melted into one vastness but a great multitude of individuals which no man can number crying with a loud voice, "Salvation to our God which sitteth upon the throne and unto the Lamb."

If Christianity is a religion of meeting, then it is proper to describe what takes place in worship as a kind of conversation, for that is the activity which belongs to meeting. Jeremiah mentions the word of the Lord as coming to him. In return he prays, "Let me talk with thee of thy judgments." It was conversation, to and fro. The Greek word for a sermon, *homilia* or homily, has the meaning of conversation: it is the talk of a man of God with men.

Worship is a kind of conversation, but it is the living kind that leads to action. When Jeremiah speaks of the word of the Lord, he does not think of it as a thing like a stick or a stone which he can accept or reject as he wishes. It is a communication so alive that it burns in his bones until he has transmitted it to those for whom it is meant. "I am weary with holding it in, and I cannot." What he cannot hold in is the *dabar* which the Lord gives him—an expression with two meanings: ordinarily "speech," "a word," it is sometimes used to mean action. The prophet says, in effect, "The Lord puts action in me." The words of conversation returned by man to God are worse than nothing if they are simply words. The only way in which man can talk to God is with his whole self, the whole living, acting self. Anything less is taking the name of God in vain. As for the relation of man to man, if the worship does not express itself in life, if cultus does not expand itself into moral code, if we hear the word of the Lord and do not *do* it, our foundation is sand.

The minister, then, who is responsible in his way for seeing that the conversation between God and man, the mutuality between man and man, goes on, is a messenger indeed. It is his to see not merely that words in the ordinary sense are delivered between God and man, and man and man, but that action is delivered from God to man and from man to man. There is nothing flat or lifeless about it. It is conversation in the round, conversation in being. It is his to see that there is meeting and ex-change of understanding between God and man, and man and man.

Only a little while ago we tried to indicate that if there is one center where all of these do meet it is in the living Christ. The minister's task then is to bring all to him, to do all in his presence.

Let us see his task as in three concentric circles.

His first task is to bring worshipers as close to Christ as he can within the context of *worship*. Here the deathless contacts which give meaning to existence are discovered and sustained.

Then there is the circle of the parish, which includes the wor-shiping congregation but finds the worshipers also in all the activities of the *life of the parish*. Here also it would seem to be his task to make Christ dominant. The relationships of God to man, and man to man, which are knit together in Christ, that is, the fundamental relationships of worship, if they are basic, should be carried to the boundaries of the parish.

Finally, these relationships should be carried to *the bound-aries of the world*.

This is the task of the minister or priest, and in all of it he is a messenger, responsible for establishing living conversations.

12. TWO DIMENSIONS OF MINISTRY

The Missionary Attitude of the Congregation

I have often heard Catholic clergy speak of the ecstasy and terror that came over them when first they performed the mass as young priests. Their belief that under their hands the bread and wine become the body and blood of God Himself gives them to feel that they are standing at the dread border where the timeless crosses over into time. But every minister or priest must have the same realization when he stands to lead public worship. At that moment he becomes the link between the age-less and unchanging things of God and the concrete actualities of every day. He may not believe that the baken dough and the fermented grape are altered in eternal texture at his word, but in worship he does see created before him the relationships, God to man, man to man, that belong to heaven. Every Christian service looks in four directions. It looks straight at the past and sees the event of Calvary. It has its eye on the *now*, and is aware of a real presence. It also turns toward the future: if any person desires to know what kind of world we should and could grow into, there it is, in principle—humanity brought together in love and mutual esteem with Christ as its center. But it is also a prefiguration of relationships which are eternal. The veil between eternity and time is broken in Christ, and the service itself is an irruption of the former into the latter. It is over this kind of event that every minister presides at every service of corporate worship.

Since it is the task of the ministrant at the service to point out to every man and to all men in their need the ageless resources of God, theology (the science of the relation of God to man), sociology (the science of the relation of man to man), and psychology (the science of the self, which is a sister to each of the others), must all have part in his ministration. The lines between God and man and those between man and man are the warp and woof of his fabric.

On the theological-psychological line, there is no substitute, as we have now said so often, for introducing the people to the one who, being in the form of God, took upon him the form of a servant and was made in the likeness of men. If the people can see him clearly, the God who hath highly exalted him will also exalt their hearts. There are, after all, only three themes in Christian theology—incarnation, atonement, and salvation— and if the minister in liturgy and sermon can provide the words in which, as an accompaniment for theophany, the great God can enter into human life at the grass roots, presently to reveal Himself here, and so to illumine life with saving meaning, the service does become a re-enactment of the divine drama.

I have no techniques whatever to offer to the minister to as- sist him in his part of this re-enactment, but if before the service, as he gets ready for it with thought and prayer, he will consider what he can do with the symbols at his command in order to prepare the way for what one might call the down-motion of incarnation, asking himself, How can God in Christ best come into my soul and that of every worshiper here? and then think of the in-motion, asking, How can I help this worshiper to know that God wishes to identify Himself with him? and then remember the end of all, the up-motion, asking, How can we best express our thanks for the saving and unspeakable gift of Himself?—if he prepares himself in this spiritual way, it is alto- gether likely that God will take his poor symbols and make them the media of a sacramental experience. He may not borrow a word from the book of theological cant (and it will be better if he does not), but all his striving will be to make straight the way for the Lord's incarnation, atonement, and salvation.

Let me take three illustrations of these themes from the ser- mons of Thomas Hooker—though it is, of course, to be under- stood that not the sermon alone but the entire service should be made to allow God in Christ to come, to give Himself, and to take to Himself. This first minister of Hartford, largely unsung as an artist for Christ in the pulpit yet among the very greatest New England has ever been able to boast, takes up the theme of incarnation in these words:

God hath appointed comfort for them that mourne, to give them beauty for ashes, the oile of joy for mourning, the garment of praise for the spirit of heavinesse. . . . Though you be poore in the world, and live in a smoakie cottage, yet the Lord will dwell with you in that poore cottage and that poore family of yours, and he will revive that poore heart of yours. . . . He that sitteth in heaven, and hath ten thousand thousand angels to minister unto him, hath but two Thrones, the highest heavens, and the lowest heart.

And here is how Hooker treats atonement between the living Christ and the living soul:

Labour to give attendance daily to the promise of grace and Christ, drive all other suitors away from the soule, and let nothing come between the promise and it, and forbid all other banes; that is, let the promise confer daily with thy heart. You know if all things be done and agreed upon betweene two parties to be married, and there wants nothing but the fixing of their affections one upon another, the onely way to draw their affections to one another is to keepe company together, and daily to meet and see one another, so as they meet wisely and holily; . . . so let thy soule daily keep company with the promise, and let not thy heart onely see the promise once in a week, but shut out all others, and keep company onely with that, and see what beauty, and strength, and grace there is in the same. Thus keep company with the promise, that thy soule and it may dwell together.

As for salvation from sin, Hooker knows that there is no substitute for putting the soul in Christ's care:

Sinne . . . challenges a title; yet Christ having taken possession, hee will have all charges; when sinne saith, I have possessed the Soule from my youth, therefore why should I out, Christ replies, it is usurped, all this title is but forged, it is mine, and I come for my owne, therefore, sinne, depart.

While I am quoting Hooker I cannot forbear citing one more passage which indicates the manner in which he believes ministers should do their work. He appeals to the messengers of Christ not to put anything less than themselves in their fullness into their message.

This is the summe of all, Ministers they doe not deliver God's word with a heavenly, hearty, and violent affection, they do not speake out of the aboundance of their affections. If they should speake against sin with a holy indignation, it would make men stand in awe of sin. They talk of it hoverly, and say, It is not good to profane God's name, and to live an ungodly life. A sturdy messenger, if he come to a mans house to speake with him, he will not be put off, he will take no deniall, but he will speake with him, if it be possible, before he goes away: but send a childe of a message to a man, if a servant doe but tell him his master is not at leisure, or that he may speake with him another time, he will easily be put off, and goe away before he hath delivered his message. So it is with a minister that performs his office with a hearty affection. He will not be dallied withall, he will take no deniall, but will have what he came for. We came to speake to your hearts, we came for hearts, and we will have hearts before we goe.

It will do none of us any harm to go to school to Thomas Hooker.

The psychological-sociological line might be called the horizontal element in corporate worship. When Christ comes in on the vertical dimension, this other is likely to take care of itself, for the love of Christ and division among men are contradictory terms.

It is recorded that in the old days when pews were owned by

the several families of a village, there was need to put a new roof
on the church in Guilford. One man refused to pay his assess-
ment on most logical grounds. "It does not leak over my pew,"
he said, and went about his business—or did he? "I must be
about my father's business," said our Lord. The site of any worshiper's business is his father's world.

The visible congregation is a microcosm of the entire church.
In Forsyth's well-known phrase, it is an outcropping of the
great church. Just as when you examine a showing of rock in an
area where the ridge lies now underground and now visible,
you will find it geologically the same as the others on the landscape and know that they are all parts of the one petrological
structure of that part of the earth's surface, so when you examine
any local church you will find it—in its essence, if it be Christian
—to be like every other. Christ is in them all, and makes all of
them one church. The rock is not Peter, but Peter's Lord. I find
this an enlarging conception, that the congregation before me in
worship is the mighty intercontinental, intergenerational church
represented in these few. Just as they here are drawn together in
Christ, so the entire church is drawn together. It is the entire
church, in principle.

What shall we say of the many beyond the boundaries of the
great church? What is our relation as worshipers to people of
other religions and of no religion? What is the attitude a minister should have and impart to his people? With your permis-
sion I shall speak of this at some little length not only because,
with the shrinking of the world, it begins to be a primary problem but because it illustrates my major emphasis, that the point
at which we can discover our best insights is that of worship.

I begin not with a worshiper's solution to this problem, but
with a philosopher's—the famous parable of the Moslem mystic,
Jalal-ed-Din Rumi, which has been told and retold in many

forms since the thirteenth century, when it first came from the lips of the author. Certain Hindus, according to the tale, brought to a city in the Middle East an elephant, and put him in an unlighted stable. Many persons who had never seen an elephant came to inspect it, but the place was so completely dark that nothing could be seen, and the visitors had to touch the animal to find out what kind of creature it was. One touched the trunk and declared that an elephant is like a tube; the one that touched the ear held that an elephant resembles a fan; the third that touched his leg was sure that an elephant is a kind of column; and finally, the man that felt of his back was sure that the form of an elephant is that of an enormous seat (for this particular elephant seems to have come complete with howdah).

So the philosopher would intimate that all beliefs have some justification and all are equally good. When people are gathered together in church, it is perfectly proper for them to believe what they believe, but it is equally proper for others to believe something quite different. Some have touched one part of the elephant of reality, others another, some no part at all, but to the philosopher they all have equally good claims.

This attitude of mind is likely to fill one with a sense of expansive magnanimity. After all, this is what the much-traveled are likely to have as their philosophy: they have seen too much of the world to settle down to the beliefs of any particular place. A sophomore at college may come to think that the beliefs which center around simple Lares and Penates, the beliefs of his parents, for instance, who perhaps never even went to college, are a bit too narrow for anybody who has the privilege of taking Philosophy 101.

People who are my age, that is, who were born in the nineteenth century, can remember when this point of view was shared by a great many educated people—and we have likewise

seen an innumerable company of our friends among these educated people grow into taking a different view of things, and
this, I believe, for two reasons.

In the first place, when they tried to make themselves believe
that all beliefs were equally good, each bringing out some aspect
of the eternal reality, they presently discovered that the beliefs
they held began to lose their value. If I say (and believe), "What
I feel is true," I find the experience positive and strengthening,
for there is hardly anything in life better than discovering the
truth, or even the tiniest part of it. But if *you* now say (and believe), "What I feel is true," and I *join* you in philosophical
amity, trying to believe that what you see is just as true for you
as what I see is true for me—truth for me being a bit of tubing,
for you a column of a hall—I find myself thinking, "Well, after
all, neither one of us sees the ultimate truth, so why get so
wrought up?" So it turns out that those that try to believe that
all beliefs are equally good find themselves believing that all
beliefs are equally bad, or equally inadequate. One might just as
well not have touched the elephant at all.

But in the second place the elephant idea of religion and our
human apprehension of it is inept because it is essentially not
honest, and therefore cannot be made to work. You who have
touched the back of the beast may try to make yourself believe,
that is, you may think you ought to believe, that the man who
has touched his ear has an equally good understanding of him,
but in your most honest moments, you will know that you de-
ceive yourself, for no person can trust the experiences of another
with quite the confidence that he can trust his own. I felt the
animal: I don't really know whether that other person felt anything or not.

Once upon a time I sat in a philosophy class as a university
undergraduate: well I remember the morning when one of my

classmates said to the teacher, "Sir, you have been telling us what Descartes and Immanuel Kant and others thought about the meaning of human life. What do *you* think?" Thereupon the professor, belonging to a school which was prevalent at the time, intimated that his task was not at all to let the student know what he thought; his views were no better than any other's, and he tried to keep himself out of his teaching. Contrast this with another professor of mine who began *his* course in philosophy by saying, "Now I mean to open to you just as accurately as I can the thought of the various men we are to study, but however objective I try to be I know in advance that my own personal predilections will show themselves. You must know therefore that I am American, a Republican who sometimes votes Democratic, brought up in the state of Ohio in a Christian home. This is my personal equation, and all my views should be corrected from it. From time to time I shall give you my views, always trying to differentiate them from those of the men we are studying, though not trying to hide my preference for my own." Which was the better method? The latter method has driven the former out of the classroom because it is more honest. A man who can say, "This is the way the animal felt to me," can quicken my mind partly because I am drawn to him as a frank human being. The man who claims or tries to claim that his touch of the animal has not really colored his thinking is simply naïve.

One of the truths we have learned in the so-called ecumenical movement is that though Congregationalists and Lutherans and the others are quite ready to be friendly to people of other denominations, they really believe that their own idea is superior to the others. This is honest—and this, I think, represents the change that has come over the Church of Christ in the last generation. At the same time that we have been developing a new reciprocity between the churches, there has been a development of the confessional groups: each one believes that his group interprets the Gospel a bit better than the others do. I find no fault with this.

Fault begins where a person moves over into fanaticism, taking the work of God into his own hands. The logic of it seems forthright enough. I possess the faith: therefore I will impart it in any way that I can. In the French Revolution the motto of some is caricatured as having been: "*Sois mon frère ou je te tue!*" Be my brother or I'll kill you! It is hard to know which is worse, the man who believes all beliefs are about the same and therefore has no real personal belief he can call his own or the one who, having his own, insists upon forcing it upon you.

I knew an institution once—an educational institution— where it was decided by a small group that everyone should become Christian. The rest were already Christians of a sort, to be sure, but not the kind that this group defined as such. So they went to work, asking the others about the state of their souls, foisting themselves and their theme into every situation. Introspection of a highly emotional type became the order of the day, and of the night. After one or two of the students went home in an overwrought nervous condition the administration called the orgy to a halt. It had become clear that if there is need to live with other people, you must take it for granted that there is an area of their inner life which is their own: you dare not invade it—and you cannot without danger to them and reactively to yourself. These are the people who have felt some part of the elephant and are jolly well going to make you feel it, or else.

What then is the situation? The figure of the elephant is wrong because it was dreamed up from a philosopher's chair and not from the pew and kneeling bench. Every worshiper knows, in the first place, that nobody ever finds God in the way that the men in the parable found the elephant. God always takes the initiative. Religion to a worshiper is never of the nature of something extra, something added to life, an elephant that Hindus have brought to town: it is always the essence of life.

If you were not a swimmer and were swept off a small boat into a lake, you would not stop to philosophize about the situation: you would not say, "Now, let me see: what is the nature of air? It is a fluid. What are its chemical components? There must be oxygen in it. Who has written the best treatise on the subject?" All you would do would be to struggle to get to the air, to breathe it, to let your lungs feel the element for which they were designed. Air is not there as a result of your discovery: you discover it in a way, but always as something given. It was here before you were. Air could exist without you, but you could not exist without it. So the Christian worshiper knows that he could not exist without God as He is revealed in Christ. You can see from this how hopelessly deficient the trope of the elephant is, for you do not need an elephant in order to exist.

The worshiper knows that God has spoken to him in Christ. He is aware that God has called him into the world for a purpose, and that he will go right if he follows it and wrong if he does not. He is fixed on a firm foundation. He is at home in God's world; and because he has all these blessings, he cannot but wish that those outside the church had them, too. Therefore he will not say, "Their beliefs are just as good as mine." Nor will he say, "I am going to change their viewpoint or know the reason why." He knows he cannot impart belief to another person. Only God by His Holy Spirit can communicate belief in God. Only God can reveal Himself to a human soul.

When Christ is present—the air to my spiritual lungs, without whom I cannot deeply live—it is love that controls my attitudes both within and beyond the church borders. You try to help others to become what God designed them to be. You are not indifferent to them, but you do not force their inner life. You witness, and let God do the rest.

This, I am convinced, is the missionary attitude that should dominate Christian thinking. There are Christians outside our denomination (whatever it may be) whose interpretation of certain doctrines is, to say it sweetly, not quite our own: what shall our attitude toward them be? Backed by our own full faith in God, duly witnessed to, can it be anything but that of Christian love? And does not the same good principle hold for those outside the Christian fold, followers after other gods and followers after none—a full faith witnessed to, and Christian love? A missionary of Christ is one who lets his own convictions be known, approaches other faiths as systems of conviction held by honored friends, and depends upon God (and not upon his own power in any form) for any conversions that may take place.

This attitude is prefigured in worship. I know no better school for preparing one for life in this horizontal—this psychological-sociological—dimension than honest, open-souled, sensitively responsive corporate Christian worship, for in that kind of worship, under God and in Christ's presence, one develops toward one's neighbor just that tension of concern and deference which marks the relationship of love. It is in this kind of worship that a minister should lead his people.

IV. Within the Parish

13. THE PROBLEM OF TRUTH

AT ONCE CERTAIN AND A DOUBTER

The minister, being a messenger aiding in the carrying on of a conversation, must be a truthful messenger. This makes it worth while to consider a problem or two having to do with the minister's, not to say the church's, relation to truth.

The first question is: How can the minister, or the church, know the truth at all? How can he be so certain about it? This is a question often put by college and university people of a sort. Indeed I think I can get into the matter best by pointing out the caricatures that church and university sometimes have of each other.

To the church the average university (apart from its scientific departments, for which there is a good deal of respect) which boasts that it will follow the truth wherever it leads, though it has no notion whither it will be lead, is comparable to a professor who has got on a train and does not know where he is going. I quote from the report of a survey of universities made by a cautious critic a few years ago:

The points upon which the student of eighteen or twenty is supposed to think for himself and come to wise decisions are precisely those upon which the college faculty as a unit is unwilling or unable to think for itself, or to come to any decision at all, wise or unwise. . . . So far as I am aware, it is only in the last century that there has been such an anomaly as an educational institution with no philosophy of life, a guide with no knowledge of the goal, or of the road to it, or even of whether or not there be a goal.

But we are more interested in what some university people think of the church. It seems to them wholly uninterested in the search for the truth—and why should it be, since it claims already to possess it? To them the church is a somewhat simple-minded lady who is committed to a set of notions, more or less outworn, and whose piety (to borrow from Chekhov) is a kind of trolley line on which she travels tiresomely back and forth. Her course has direction, God wot, but is wholly without creative deviation:

> All our fathers have been churchmen
>   Nineteen hundred years or so
> And to every new suggestion
>   They have always answered "No."

It behooves us to take this conception of the church, though a travesty, with all seriousness. How can we claim that we have the truth? I think that, at least for the Protestant, the answer is simple enough, and again it is found in the consciousness of the worshiper.

An insight of Martin Luther, which he imparted to the world, is brought out in the phrase, *simul justus et peccator,* descriptive of the paradoxical state in which a redeemed man finds himself "justified although a sinner." Luther's dilemma is every man's dilemma. On the one hand, according to the justice of this world, no man can be justified who lives in sin, and yet we all live in sin: there is no getting out of it. No man is perfect. But here Luther's great moment dawned. He saw that God had taken the initiative and by an act of forgiveness, made brilliant and terrifying in Christ, had broken through the karma-like chain of justice in which men found themselves fettered. That changed the look of things. No longer did the future rest for any man upon his own deeds, important though they are in their place. The forgiveness in the heart of the Cosmic Judge was the ultimate matter: thence would come the last word. There is an eschatological element here: God has justified us in such a way that, though we are now in sin, at the last, thanks to God's forgiveness, already displayed, we shall be found to be not in sin. The result of living in such a paradox is gratitude, and we try in gratitude to throw our sins off.

When this paradoxical consciousness is translated into the realm of truth, as the worshiper knows it, the phrase to parallel the *simul justus et peccator* is *simul certus et dubitator*—for here the redeemed man, the man to whom God has come in Christ, is "certain in the midst of his doubts." Here the dilemma is not unlike that which Luther found in the moral sphere. On the one hand, according to the wisdom of the world, no man can be wise who lives in ignorance, and yet we all live in ignorance: there is no getting out of it. No man is omniscient. We live in a cloud of unfinality: who can escape it? We know that if a thought could be found which explained everything else it would be its own insoluble problem, but here a corollary of Luther's insight is to the fore. Again is seen the significance of God's taking the initiative: in a humanly hopeless situation, by an act of revelation (for it is nothing less) as part of the grace made manifest in Christ he breaks through the chain of relativity by which men are bound. This changes one's attitude toward learning and truth. No longer does the future rest for any man upon his own knowledge. Even Copernican systems can be overthrown. That God knows and will ultimately disclose all things is the important matter. There is an eschatological moment here, too: God has revealed that though we do not know today, there will come a *then* when we shall know even as also we are known. The result of this paradoxical state of affairs is that, for the Christian, the acquisition of information is not a hopeless attempt to know all, but a life of gratitude in companionship with the great Knower in the course of which we try to throw off all the ignorance we can.

As a good messenger, therefore, that is, a truthful one, the minister is as certain of God who reveals Himself to him in the living Christ as he is ready to be an inquirer about all created things. If one asks whether he is committed to some form of truth, his answer is an unequivocal affirmative. He does not believe he must wait until tomorrow—tomorrow and tomorrow and tomorrow, creeping in this petty pace to the last syllable of recorded time—to learn what kind of world this is. The God who presides over the universe, being among other things a Knower who is friendly to learning, will one day by His grace receive men to Himself as knowers. On the other hand, if one asks whether the Christian minister is an indoctrinator, who transmits unexamined material to his people, the answer is an unambiguous negative. He is an inveterate inquirer into all things which can be viewed and handled, including beliefs about God. That is to say, he is a fixed *believer* in God as He reveals Himself in the living Christ but a critical *examiner* of all of God's dealing with us in His universe. If he is a truthful messenger, this will be his attitude.

During the last century the chapel at Harvard has given a fascinating illustration of the narrowness of the ridge on which the man at once certain and a doubter has to walk, and how easy it is for him to slip down on one side or the other. I have the history from Dr. Elliott Perkins, whose family has known Harvard intimately for many a generation. Charles Francis

Adams of the class of 1856 gives us an idea of what Sabbath observance was like in his boyhood:

How I disliked Sunday. . . . I remember now the silence, the sombre idleness, the sanctified atmosphere of restraint of those days, with their church bells, their sedate walk, and their special duties. After breakfast came Bible reading, four chapters, each of us four verses in rotation. Then a Sunday lesson, committing some verses from the Bible or a religious poem to memory. Then came the going to church. Lord! That going to church! Twice a day, rain or shine, summer and winter!

In a word, there was certainty enough. Undoubtedly the one living standard of the Lord Jesus Christ was there, but he had become so completely frozen in among dreary symbols that had themselves taken the place of the unchanging Lord to whom they were supposed to point that there was no thought of inquiring into and possibly improving them.

The situation was similar, according to some, in the Divinity School. It was in 1853 that Theodore Parker wrote a letter which we sometimes read to each other at today's Divinity School for our soul's good. He compares theological education to the process of mummification:

I was over at Cambridge the other day and looked in at the Divinity School, & saw several of the *Bodies* which were waiting their turn. The operators were not in at the time so I saw nothing of the *modus operandi*. The Aegyptian Embalmers took only seventy days I think to make a mummy out of a dead man. [The] Embalmers [here] use three years in making a mummy out of live men.

Of the graduates of a seminary he writes:

Pitch, Gum, Asphaltum—had never done their work better. There stood the mummies dead & dry as Shishak, ready to be ordained & put up in a—Pulpit.

It was by men who remembered the childhood Adams described and the chapel service at the college (another exercise in imposed monotony), and who knew something of the Divinity School, that in 1886, when Mr. Perkins' grandfather, Charles William Eliot was President, compulsory chapel was abolished; and the member of the Board of Overseers who was the strongest advocate of the revolutionary act was Phillips Brooks.

Then followed a religious heyday at Harvard. There were of course those worshipers of the past who thought that Harvard had voted out God, and told the public press as much, but actually the public worship there was greatly strengthened for the time. An Edinburgh divine who in 1887 had visited eight compulsory chapel services in as many colleges and then come to Cambridge said that the service in the Yard was "the most religious . . . public or private" that he had attended on his tour.

But in their new-found freedom to inquire and alter, the religious community seems to have neglected the one thing needful—basic belief. They voted out the living Christ, along with all the symbols. The idea which seems presently to have won the day is summed up in the phrase: "No commitments to anything." This attitude of mind, along with other elements in the *Zeitgeist,* in a generation produced the normal chapel scene of the 1920's. George Weller of 1929 writes in an autobiographical note, "The bell was ringing for morning chapel. Seven men out of seven thousand attended."

Today there are many times seven in the morning service at chapel, even on the leanest days, and surely one of the reasons why is that it is now a place *both* of commitment *and* of inquiry. It is Christ, the reality through which God awakes a man to His presence, who is the standard to which commitment is made. But in the light that he sheds on life, all symbols are inquired into, judged, and if need be altered.

The Protestant minister as a bearer of truth is *certain* of the God and Father of our Lord Jesus Christ, whom he meets in an I-thou relationship, but he *inquires* about all things in the world and checks them against his certitude. This is the mood of worship.

14. A PROBLEM OF TRANSMITTING TRUTH

Subjecting Symbols to Criticism

Since symbols, which we use in our worship to help us maintain our attention upon God, must be correlated with the object to which they refer, as we have pointed out, it is clear that they must be submitted to a relentless criticism. We do not want to associate God with anything unworthy of Him. The minister of Christ must defend Him against inadequate symbols. In this field we must put all the tools of science into the service of faith. That indeed is the highest use to which they can be put.

We do not accept that view of truth as once for all delivered to the saints which impelled the particular army of Moslems who took Alexandria to burn to ashes its priceless library on the ground that all truth could be found in its final form in the Koran. On the contrary, to us the essential and abiding element, at the source of and lending meaning to all life, is God, who, though He has spoken to us supremely in Jesus Christ, still speaks in many ways. Our symbols, to be kept alive, must constantly be under what we believe to be His judgment—and nowhere else is more exactly illustrated the dictum that judgment gives life.

The institution which can make a place for criticism of itself is alive. If the symbols used are under the judgment only of the church, the church itself tends to usurp the place of God. The great gift of Protestantism to the world, as it is now seen to be emerging, is its pure faith in God alone, which makes it willing to submit even the church itself to His judgment. To God be Glory—and no glory to the church except as God chooses the church to reflect His glory. We are very confident that the Lord hath more truth and light to break forth out of His holy word, but in order to know that we are properly interpreting this truth and light, we require all the aids that science can give us.

Men of my age can remember how timidly some leaders in the church took up the tools of research that advancing science put into their hands. "They are secular tools: use them therefore on all things secular, but keep them away from the Bible—or if the Bible is to be laid on the laboratory table, remember that the divinity of our Lord makes the story of his own life sacrosanct." Today we know how silly those fears were. Now that we have fully entered the world of criticism, which is ready with its various test tubes and retorts to assess everything, literally everything that the hand of man can touch or his eye see or his ear hear, we do not find that we have displaced the throne of God by the minutest millimeter. He is still where He was when the foundations of the earth were laid, when its measures were laid, and the morning stars sang together. He is still revealed in Jesus Christ, and as for the earthly life of Christ, we know it far better than our fathers did, and, as I have already suggested, even though we admit the possibility that some discovery might be made which would cause us to revise our knowledge of his comings and goings, the severest inquest into text and history at this point verifies rather than contradicts our belief. Nothing is more certain than that God is a God of loving concern: this we can identify by the power with which He seizes our hearts. Demonstration of Him beyond this is somewhat superfluous, but every law of causality on which science rests would seem to suggest that the church's memory of this God's entering history has a historical basis. I believe that one of the reasons for the upsurge of interest in religion in this country is the feeling that the Thirty Years' War between religion and science is well over, and the new Peace of Westphalia opens up a magnificent era for both.

To all the symbols used by man in his worship we are ready to apply the most corrosive scientific tests. Let me put in English words a famous definition of Willamowitz-Mollendorff, but to preserve its delightful flavor, at once Teutonic and scientific, let me keep the German order:

The so-called strict philological method this means simply the undeviatingly honest, in great things as in small no-difficulty-shunning, no-doubt-glozing-over, no-gap-in-the-record-or-in-our-own-knowledge-covering-up, always to oneself and others account-rendering, search for truth.

This is the way Protestantism at its freest and best keeps its symbols in review. Symbols theological (words, ideas, philosophies), symbols liturgical (including all the expressions of music and the other arts), symbols political (the various ecclesiastical organizations viewed as training grounds or instruments for expressing Christian love) are each in their own way under God's judgment. The whole human side of the church and everything that is in it is therefore to be looked at by man in such light as he understands God's judgment to shed. The lens of science is man's contraption for searching into things as they are, that is, into God's understanding of things.

Alas, then, one may say, we shall never find the perfect symbol, since we can never penetrate to the inner area of things, understanding them as God does: all symbols shimmer in tentativeness. Now if we had to depend upon the absolute standing of a symbol to support the absoluteness of God, we should indeed find any symbol a weak reed; but let us remember that a symbol is only something that man uses to help him keep his attention upon God in the hope, based upon precedent, that God will make of it a sacrament and through it enter the heart of the worshiper. To serve as such, an object does not need to be mined from the basic magma of reality itself, but the worshiper does need to bring it to the Lord with the spirit of truthfulness. It must check with reality as the worshiper knows reality, else he is taking God's name in vain. To ask God to accept a symbol which does not agree with your own sense of reality is to despise Him as a judge. The statement of belief must be honest; the myth must carry the truth; the architecture must sing the praise of God and not extol confusion or human sentiment; the Boy Scout troop must be conducted for the benefit of the boys on behalf of him who said, "Suffer the little children to come unto me." If the symbol makes toward what we conceive to be reality, expect God to use it as a sacrament; but this entails the continuous process of comparing symbols with reality—in short, unending research. The false idols will finally topple and fall before man's meddling intellect: those which God can use will remain.

In the language of worship, this is to say that all our symbols are under the judgment of Him to whom they are designed to point. When God completes worship by His own touch, when He speaks sacramentally to the soul, as He chiefly does through Jesus Christ, disclosing His character of love, the veil is off the face of reality, and everything else associated with our worship and with our lives must be judged, and is judged, by Him who is thus disclosed. Every single symbol must be made to accord with His reality.

15. OTHER PROBLEMS OF TRANSMITTING TRUTH

CAN A LIAR TELL THE TRUTH OR A TRUTH-TELLER LIE?

For the minister as a messenger of truth two further moral problems emerge. The first of these belongs to yesterday rather than today. When Protestants looked back at the kind of Catholicism which they had just left in the sixteenth century, they knew that there was many a priest who did not believe the truth of the Gospel, or at least did not live it. He might even be nine parts of a scoundrel. The elaborate series of fabrications and forgeries beginning in the sixth century with the *Liber Pontificalis* and continuing into the Middle Ages were doubtless all the handiwork of men ordained to be priests of the church. Hildebrand's theocracy, brilliant with hope at the beginning, had degenerated into a "secular dominion exercised by worldly men for worldly ends." The pretended Pope John, for instance, had found his way to the exalted seat of Peter by way of the gentle craft of piracy. The question then was as to whether the pure truth of the Gospel could be conveyed through hands such as theirs: could it be transmitted by impure carriers?

There are few today who would say that the truth could not be so conveyed, and this no more by virtue of the historical fact that it has, than on the principle that no man's hands are clean, that sin separates even the most saintly minister of Christ from perfection, and that therefore the Gospel must have in itself a certain power of continuing identity which cannot quite be removed from it even by unworthy transmitters. This is a source of reassurance to all ministers.

On the other hand, as every Protestant and Catholic priest and minister would surely insist, the centrality of Christ is

better exhibited by a saintly life, his work better done by a servant who is dedicated to his truth, than by those who in the
fashion of the Assyrian, the rod of God's anger, or in some
kindred way, do His will in spite of themselves.

Good. If we say then that though it is undesirable and offen-
sive it is still possible for a minister or priest who does not
believe in the truth to transmit it, shall we now go on to assert
that one who believes is justified in transmitting what he regards as untrue? This is our second problem.

The question is as to whether a lover of God's truth can transmit a lie in such a way as will actually reveal truth. Here the
mise en scène is the tradition of public worship of which a part
has come to be recognized as false. An error, say, has appeared
in the tradition: should you perpetuate it for good reasons?
For illustration let us cite the phrase "born of the Virgin Mary,"
in the Apostles' Creed. If you believe that Jesus was as a historical fact born of a virgin, you have no problem at this point. But
suppose you have come to the conclusion that the argument
from the silence of St. Paul and of Mark and Q and other considerations drawn from the Biblical text are final; or suppose
that you see in the doctrine an expression of the Monophysite
heresy before Chalcedon—and who will hold that a completely
human person could have been born without a human father?—
and so, for one reason or another, you feel that the teaching is
not part of the Gospel, or is a false and extraneous element in
the tradition, what then? Do you as a minister lead the creed for
the rest of the church to follow? Are you performing your func-
tion as an accurate transmitter of the things of God if you do so?
Can you do this as a worshiper of the God of truth?

This brings a new factor into our equation. The minister is
not only the transmitter of the things of the people through
Christ to God and the things of God through Christ to the

people. He is also one of a company of transmitters. He is a member of a line. He acts not merely as an individual but as one of a team. If he speaks a word of transmission different from that which has been spoken before him, the trumpet of the church gives an uncertain sound and listeners are more likely to hear confusion than they are to hear the Gospel. People will turn away from the church, with the untoward result that neither the minister's version of the Gospel nor any other will be heard. Or confusion and controversy will ensue to such an extent that the fruit of the church will be not love, joy, and peace, but antagonism, unhappiness, and spiritual war. Will a minister truly represent Christ if that is the effect his message produces?

The course to pursue in such a situation is that which must be resorted to by any innovator in any society. Without forfeiting his own confidence in the revelation which has come to him, he must surely give decent regard to the opinions of others. He cannot with impunity ride roughshod over the time-honored beliefs of his fellow Christians. Christian love forbids this. He can, however, set about changing them, if he is certain they are wrong. It is only after he is assured that by and large the company to whom he is responsible will understand and participate in the change that he will make it. If he is the minister of a church in which the form of worship is in the care of the local congregation, his task, if the other leaders and people of the church will make their studies toward truth with him, is relatively easy. If, however, the authority in his communion is more diffused, he will obviously have to move more slowly. During this interim while he continues to lead in a form in which he does not believe but in which other Christians have obviously believed, he will try to make clear, to all, his ambiguous position wherein he continues to recite a phrase, to him false, for the good of the church's solidarity, but does so reluctantly because he loves the truth.

Time was, and perhaps still is, when the Church of England would freely allow its clergymen to deny the warning clauses of the Athanasian Creed (the very name of which is deceitful), though it would not allow them to omit the clauses from the service. This delightfully English way of straddling a difficulty suggests that some similar way may be found when an individual minister finds himself conscientiously bound to deny a part of the tradition of the church in the period before he has persuaded the rest of the church that he is right.

The abomination of desolation enters the church when a man tries to take himself off the horns of the dilemma by persuading himself that the lie is somehow right. I find even so careful a man as Berdyaev saying, "What is false for individual conscience and consciousness is changed into truth by the collective consciousness because it promotes the power of the collectivity." If this is a fair translation of his original words, it would seem to be a means of delivering the thought of the church into the hands of John of Damascus or Peter the Lombard forever. Let free-ranging minds (like that of Berdyaev himself) play upon the things of religion: the church itself in its liturgical life remains impervious to change. He who makes all things new can bring His life-giving influence to bear on everybody save His church. The church becomes the aged grandmother of civilization and sits then in her corner mumbling memories of her girlhood but with the juices of growth now dried in her brittle arteries.

To say that what is a lie for an individual may become a truth for a collectivity reminds me of the statement of Judge Lawless in 1836 in excusing the burning to death of a Negro, Francis L. McIntosh, by a St. Louis mob. He said that the motive was "a mysterious, metaphysical, and almost electric phrenzy" and therefore "beyond the reach of human law." The morality which governs individuals could not apply to the crowd. Is not the church really beyond this kind of thinking?

Or an untruth will be left permanently in the ritual on the ground that this is a lesser evil than separating oneself from the past. Sometimes one hears a man say, "I of course do not accept the doctrine of the Virgin Birth, but the saying of the creed which contains the reference unites me to the ancient church, so liturgically I say I believe it, though actually I do not." As if this were the only link with the ancient church! And as if an outmoded belief were a worthy link to hold the Church of Christ together!

Or it may be said that this particular doctrine of the Virgin Birth is a good myth to illustrate the dual nature of our Lord's person. This and other theological rationalizations are interesting and illuminating. There is nothing to be said against them as such. We who have lived since Freud know that the wishes are incorrigible in making the mind their accomplice, but this only sets us on our guard against their misuse. Most of us believe that myths are indispensable. But at the moment we are not considering this subject: we are asking whether an honest minister can transmit what he conceives to be false. The question is whether an honest minister could with moral impunity transmit a bad myth. As a matter of fact I believe the story of the Virgin Birth, if regarded as a myth, must be held to be a bad one. It conceives our Lord as partly human, partly divine, whereas the catholic faith as I understand and hold it conceives him wholly human and wholly divine. Can a minister communicate the catholic faith by means of a myth which he regards as uncatholic?

I do not argue that we should turn away from the past or

even that we should shut out from our worship myths with strains of badness in them. Let us not reject romance and any of the imaginative arts. Let us tell the Christmas story forever as early generations told it, but let us tell it as to ourselves in the mood of children, as in the atmosphere of the church's childhood. There is a place for this in the church and even in the worship itself. There is no end of historical material in the sermon, in the reading of the Bible, and in many other places in the liturgy which is not part of the firm core of permanent belief and which no worshiper takes to be such. A parable used in preaching, a Scripture passage read at random and uncritically, the words of many a hymn—these find their legitimate place in the service; and not being heralded by the declaration *credo*— I believe!—they do not jeopardize integrity.

A creed, however, is a statement of quintessential belief. The congregation should recite it standing at attention (as Studdert-Kennedy said), and facing the altar of the God of truth. Most of us can do that when we say, "We believe in God the Father almighty, maker of heaven and earth, and in Jesus Christ his only son our Lord." These facts are beyond the inquiry of historians. Others of you may feel that the reference to the Virgin Birth is equally well revealed. I speak only of the minister who does *not* believe that this is a matter for the historian rather than the theologian. I am hoping that he will never be able to recite in a credo what to him is untrue without some twinge of conscience and without pledging himself to have that changed some day in order that the Church of Jesus Christ may be pure. I am speaking of course of a minister who has at least some ultimate responsibility for the content of the services of his church and not of a person who is a guest in the church of others, where Christian considerations would seem to argue that he make himself as unobtrusive as possible.

I know what hesitation there is on almost every hand to changing the articles of the church's worship. It was an Anglican friend who pointed out to me years ago that when the official photographer had marshaled the serried ranks of bishops outside of Lambeth Palace in the first days of one of the conferences he warned them, "Now remember, any movement spoils the group!" Worth remembering are the words of Froude:

If medicine had been regulated three hundred years ago by Act of Parliament; and if there had been Thirty-Nine Articles of Physic, and every licensed practitioner had been compelled, under pains and penalties, to compound his drugs by the prescriptions of Henry the Eighth's physician, Dr. Butts, it is easy to conjecture in what state of health this country would at present be found.

As a matter of fact there was probably a good deal in the medical theory and practice of Dr. Butts which has not been changed to this day and will probably never be changed—pure air, for instance, being just as good for a patient now as it was then. But this is not to say that there has not been improvement —and shall we set up a system of thought which encloses the tradition in such hallowed precincts that no breath of newness can ever reach it?

> Myself when young did eagerly frequent
> Doctor and Saint, and heard great argument
> About it and about; but evermore
> Came out by the same door as in I went.

Is the race as a whole going to do that? Though George Bernard Shaw had a lot to learn about the church, we can hardly resist applauding him when he says: "A church that has not enough spiritual energy to cut the dead wood out of its ritual, and lead its people instead of lagging centuries behind, is no real church at all." I believe that the churches we represent keep at the task of pruning and improving most of the time, but there seem to be times when some of them need encouragement.

Many of you young men who have been brought up in the churches of the Middle West, some of them quite homespun and unpolished, are subtly attracted to our mellower communions in the East and in the greater cities; but do not let ecclesiastical prestige blind you. A church can become so mellowed as to be mildewed. There is a place for all sorts: it was, after all, little unsophisticated groups that took the initiative against slavery, that have tried to keep Christ's will central in their social concerns, that on the whole never developed any silly theories to the effect that a lie in a liturgy is something less impure than when found elsewhere, and so share in our hope for the future. I think I speak for all communions at their best when I ask you not to let go the purity of your unsophistication.

> Truth is a maid whom men woo diversely;
> But woe to him that takes the immortal kiss
> And estates her not in his housing life,
> Mother of all his seed! So he betrays
> Not truth, the unbetrayable, but himself;
> And with his kiss . . . so consummates his Judasry.

In the Church of Jesus Christ there is no substitute for dogged veracity, even though in face of the inviolable nature of social law it may under circumstances be delayed in expression.

In a word, the leader of public worship in the church, keeping himself a true minister of Jesus Christ, the way, the life, and also the truth, must care for truth as the holy thing which it is. He must be positively eschatological in his concern for it: if he does not tell the truth as he counts upon having it verified when the sea of history shall give up its dead and the secrets of all hearts shall be disclosed, he cannot hope that his words will reflect the eternal. He may manage to stimulate conversation with the church of the past, which cherished the same untruths as the minister now repeats, but that is not what living worship is designed for: in worship it is conversation with the Most High that we desire.

16. BRINGING THE RELATIONS ESTABLISHED IN WORSHIP INTO THE TOTAL PARISH

Two Illustrations

We have already spoken of the concentric circles of the church's concern. There is the central circle of corporate worship, there is the life of the larger parish, and finally that of the great church beyond, which is made up of one's own and the other communions, and ministers to the world.

When now we step into a consideration of parish life, it is with the idea that the entire parish should be built up on the relationships established and developed in public worship. The parish thereupon becomes an area of conflict of a sort, for it is there that the centrifugal tides washing out from the point where God meets man, and man meets man, in worship, strike the waves of secularity which wash in from the outside world, threatening to engulf all. Quietly, week after week, the church pours into its parishes through its services of worship the power to acknowledge a standard in human life and courage to adhere to it. Happily some of this overflows into the community outside, but for the moment we are thinking of the parish alone. In the systole and diastole of worship the spirit of Christ flows out into the parish, or ought to, and, wherever it goes, establishes the relationships of which we have already spoken and to which we have repeatedly returned. Indeed, since he is, as we have said, the very incarnation of these relationships, we can almost take them for granted and focus our consideration on him. To make him Lord is to acknowledge these relationships—that God comes to man in creative love, that man responds in loving obedience, and that man and man are united as brethren under God.

Let us consider two aspects of the life of the parish and ask how we might bring them closer to the mind of Christ which is made clear in church worship. Here I borrow from the practices of our New England fathers.

First, the meeting of the parish for business: how can it be Christified (to use the imaginative word of a French theologian)?

In the old days of New England the business meeting of the church or of any of its committees (though the number of committees in those days was mercifully few) was conceived to take place in the presence of the living Christ. There was an atmosphere of public worship there. Now I do not think we are so far behind our ancestors at this point as might be expected in our kind of society. It is true that the memory of a single meeting of the congregation of the variety hinted at in Robert Benchley's "Treasurer's Report and Other Aspects of Community Singing" eclipses our recollection of many better meetings. But usually the business is conducted in a way becoming the dignity and purpose of the church. I believe, however, that we could improve the average meeting if the minister (especially the minister, though not only he) would do all in his power to keep the group aware that the real presiding officer is Christ.

Those who are met there are members of the church. They have covenanted with Christ and the other members to walk together in his ways and together to seek his mind concerning everything, and most especially the uses of their money—the acid test of churchmanship. These are people who worship together, who together acknowledge God's providence in prayer and praise. They have together heard the word read and preached, and lifted up their voices in many a response and hymn. Now the redemptive experience of worship merges without losing itself in the responsibility for discussing and making the best human decision concerning the things of Christ's church. Where, more than this, is it necessary to put one's free mind under the guidance of the Holy Spirit?

How the minister and his people can make the business meeting an object for the eyes of Christ they themselves will best know. It will come naturally to those who remember that the business meeting is a *church* meeting. Anything to break down the barrier between the realities encountered in worship and those of the business in hand! If the hymn, prayers, and Bible reading at the beginning are simply devices to divert attention from those who come in late, they are hardly the instruments to prepare the company for its work that they should be. If minister and people will keep in mind that even in business affairs they are waiting upon Christ, their attitudes will show it.

Given the right understanding of the realities involved, the effect will be visible both on *how* the business is conducted and on *what* the business is. My guess is that if the company felt itself to be the group appointed to carry out the will of Christ, a way would be found to dispose rather quickly of routine matters, in order to get at the matters which have a direct and more creative effect upon Christ's potential kingdom. The rules for a good church business meeting are simple:

1. Face a problem. If no problem is involved, the best creative business brains of the company are not summoned into action.

2. Face a problem which, on the one hand, is susceptible of being understood as being of concern to Christ. At this point the whole world swims into consideration, for Christ, though the governing member of every parish, is anything but parochial.

3. Face a problem which, on the other hand, is susceptible of being solved at least in part by the company present. Most of the problems of the greater church resist solution in any one parish but can be solved by many parishes working upon them independently. Consider Christ's work of compassion in foreign missions, home missions, and in the neighborhood: the quality of this mercy is as the gentle rain from heaven, but rain is made up of drops, and the drops in this case are the intelligent decisions to aid made in the various parishes as a result of the study of the need. I never cease to be impressed with the effectiveness of those churches which, at some point in their parish life, succeed in emerging from routine to consider what Christ wishes them to do in the new day.

4. Prepare in advance by studying the issues of the problem. There has been an idea abroad for a long time, due to a misunderstanding of Scripture, that the Holy Spirit will always put it into a man's mouth what to say when occasion arises, but it is noticeable that the Holy Spirit seems to succeed better where he has a few ideas inside the man's head to choose from. Even the Spirit cannot create wisdom out of ignorance.

5. Finally, remember always that the whole purpose of the meeting is to discover the mind of Christ on the problem involved.

I believe that simply by taking a little consecrated thought we may deliver the business meetings of the parish from the category of the secular and restore them, if they need restoring, to the category to which they belong, holy gatherings under the leadership of Christ, instinct with the virtues which are the spiritual structure of public worship.

In other words, the mental image of the church which is formed in worship—the loving, giving, creative God; receiving and obedient souls; God's gracious gifts being shared by their recipients with each other and insofar as possible with all mankind; and all under the judging but benign presence of Christ—this image, carried into the most practical of business meetings, may avail to make even that creative, and in its way inspiring, and broadly useful.

Another point at which we might make parish life agree more perfectly with the relations Christ brings to us in corporate worship lies in the preparation and setting apart of officers and members.

One of the striking features of old New England ecclesiastical practice was the insistence of the leaders that the people could not appoint their ministers and office-bearers. Some of you who remember well that democracy ruled these early churches and that they opposed the appointment of ministers by any other than the people of the several congregations will wonder if I correctly put the negative in the preceding sentence. The people *did* vote upon their ministers, but they did not vote to elect. They voted to nominate to Christ: he alone could make the appointment and it was to him, not to the people, that the minister was responsible. The ordination was the sign that they believed he had appointed his minister.

It will be seen that this procedure sets a standard by no means for a congregational or presbyterial system of ordination alone. It suggests something also for ordination by bishops and indeed for the consecration of bishops themselves. It has meaning as well for the choice of office-bearers of the lay order. To emphasize it would be to quicken our churches into a true apprehension of relationships within them. Most of all it could be applied to the entrance of members into the church. Who on being received as a member in the church would not be given a better awareness of what he was doing if he were told, not that the rite of "joining" or the right hand of fellowship from the elder or the touch of the bishop's hand made him the member, but that these were only the signs and seals of the admission given him by Christ himself to his church. In most churches that I know this is already the theory: I am asking only that the theory be brought out of its implicitness, lighted with practice, and made to illumine our contemporary church life as I believe it does not.

In corporate worship we acknowledge that it is only God who can create. He is the source, we are the recipients and channels, of His grace. The secularization of the church begins at the point where we forget these relationships and substitute our own, such as the idea that we need no help whatever in the creation of the office-bearers of the church. The best defense against all forms of secularizing in a local church is the influence of warm and understanding corporate worship overflowing into every area of the parish.

These two illustrations will perhaps suffice to indicate the kind of emphasis I believe can be made in every parish, and must be made, to keep the tides of secularity from washing into the church. It is a matter of letting Christ, through whom God has spoken to the race and may be expected to go on speaking, rule in all our parish doings—a matter of making the worship experience remain with us as a governing afterimage in all other meetings. In Christ's presence, God and the worshiper and humanity assume their eternal relationships, and what is done is done on solid ground.

I can almost hear someone saying, "But is not this appeal to a kind of mystical presence the fol-de-rol which in other religions we should be inclined to call superstition?" After all, what difference is there *between* getting your church business done as well as you can without bothering with theological implications *and* considering that you are doing it as a response to the will of Christ? What distinction is there *between* electing an officer or member to his place and so installing him *and* nominating him to Christ and then confirming what is believed to be the election and installation of Christ? Why not make your parish the best community you can, using all the tested principles of good social work, without dragging in the relationships to Christ? Why bother about those basic relationships which you feel reflect the eternal?

The answer to this is the answer to the whole question of the Christian life. In a sense the church brings nothing new into the world but transforms everything. The laws of physics remain the same for the Christian as for the atheist, as do the laws of politics and sociology and all the other laws of nature, but they are given a new meaning.

Analogies here are imperfect and therefore dangerous, but it is true that a radio set turned in one direction can pick up more signals than the same set pointed in another direction, because the built-in antenna is better oriented to the source of the signals. In rough similarity a church not consciously oriented toward what it remembers to have been a source of sacramental power may carry out its work pedestrianly, but that church through which the voice of Christ sings, in part because it is turned toward him, is surely more exciting to the soul in its heavenly dimension. I hope you all know Arnold Kenseth:

> As Blake saw in a tree
> Branches of wings, painted a hidden choir;
> So I write down the versions of my joy,
> Because these holy ones guest in my heart,
> Wander my blood, make my glad bones employ
> Themselves deft and daily in the earnest art
> Of adoration.

It is this joining of the two awarenesses—on the one hand the commonplace, the tree, the treasurer's report, the roll of church members, and on the other hand the divine interest, the branches of wings, Christ in the chairman's seat, Christ the ordainer—that keeps a church at once on the ground and in the heights.

The whole tendency of Continental philosophical thought today seems to be toward the acceptance of what the Germans call the *Lebenswelt,* the world of one's total life; this is a denial of every attempt to crowd life into a particular category, scientific, philosophical, which, useful in its place, is yet an abstraction. The urging is to get at the whole of life from which these abstractions are drawn. To define a congregation in social terms alone is to make it a pale abstraction of its true self.

In this light I am saying that the whole life of the church lies between the pole of God in Christ and that of the complex of details which is the everyday life of the parish. Because the supernatural cannot invade the natural in such a way as to alter the laws of the latter— causing the eyelids of the statues of the saints to wink, producing sanctification over and above the zone of the moral law, and the like—secularity constantly asks why we need the sacred. Is not Dr. Coué's "Every day in every way I'm getting better and better" as good as any "positive Christian thinking" you ever heard of? Is not the technique of the non-Christian psychiatrist as good as that of a Christian? Are the moral laws of the church society any different from those of society in general? Yes and no. The techniques are the same, but there is an incandescence of meaning in the work of the Christian that is not seen in that of the irreligious. To enter the church is not to make one's exit from the human race and all the flesh is heir to; it does not exempt one from moral responsibilities and failures; though one becomes *justus* he remains, alas, *peccator*. The difference lies in the new consciousness. If a church, while remaining in the world, knows that it is the concern of one who has overcome the world, it has air to breathe which, though unseen, imparts vigor.

That this is a right idea is supported by the experience of common worship, for everyone who worships knows that he lives simultaneously in a finite and in a transcendent world. I could properly be called a liar if I should say that there is no concrete world about me, and equally a liar if in the moment of worship I should say that my entire world is bounded by dimensions of space and time. God is not one whose weight adds a single milligram to the scales; His extent or speed of passage is not measurable in any way; and yet no physical thing is as close as He. Ears He has not, though we rightly pray to Him, and from Him we draw power, though He is not a source of voltage. Our need in our total parish life is to bring this consciousness of salvation in Christ, which is the basis of our worship together, over into the rest of the life of the parish, to reproduce the relationships which Christ induces. This is the hallmark of a true church.

V. Ecumenicity

17. BEYOND THE PARISH

THE ECUMENICAL CIRCLE

The circle of Christian concern beyond the parish is a complicated one, made up in itself of many circles. I do not stop to consider the circle of the larger church or denomination, though the relationships visible in corporate worship are alone those which make a communion viable. I want to come now to the circle in which almost all denominations are pooling new and mounting interests—that of Christian ecumenicity, "the great new fact of our time"—and apply to it solutions which derive from those same relationships. These I believe are the guideposts for all Christian enterprise.

Before we leave the local parish behind entirely, however, let us mark once more how all-important it is and how its importance lies in the fact that here, more than at any other point in the great church, are brought to light in corporate worship the fundamental relationships which avail in heaven as on earth. It can never be too strongly emphasized that ecumenicity begins at home.

There was a medieval doctrine that the soul is in the body in such a way that it is completely in every part of the body. So God, revealing Himself in Christ, is in every part of the great church: so He is completely in every congregation. The parable of the laborers in the vineyard might be retold in terms of acreage rather than time. The householder might have been represented as engaging all the men at the same time but giving one group charge of a piece of land as large as a diocese or conference, another one as large as an association or presbytery, and a third one as small as a parish, the story closing with the words of Scripture slightly changed:

So when even was come, the lord of the vineyard saith unto his steward, Call the laborers and give them their hire, beginning from the man who tilled the least acreage unto the man who tilled the most. And when the former came, they received every man a penny. But when the latter came they supposed that they should receive more; and they likewise received every man a penny. And when they received it they murmured against the good man of the house, saying, These others have wrought on but a single acre, and thou hast made them equal unto us, which have borne the burden and heat of many. But he answered one of them and said, Friend, I do thee no wrong: didst thou not agree with me for a penny? Take that thine is and go thy way: I will give unto this other, even as unto thee.

You cannot multiply Christ. He is One, and just as completely available in the one-acre congregation as in the ecclesiastical seat that looks out over thousands of acres. He can best be known in the large by a person who has met him in the intimate relationships of the local parish. Let us recall once more that many great movements of reform have come from small groups. Most of us have been given our keys to the kingdom in a local parish. The great church comes into being by the touch of God's Holy Spirit upon the hearts of men who recognize in Christ the answer to their deep desires and allow their sympathy and assistance to go out to their fellow men in Christian love; and the locus of this event is, generally speaking, the village church, or the town or city or neighborhood church. The water which forms the great river of the church, inundating and refreshing every land, takes its rise in the little local springs. With this thought in mind we turn to the ecumenical scene.

Señor de Madariaga's dictum—"We created far too much church for the faith that there was"—probably tells the truth. At any rate, the western church of the Middle Ages finally toppled and fell into pieces, and now we are in search of the kind of faith that will put it together again. At what points have we added "too much church"? Where have we so seriously adulterated the essentials as to have caused the breaks? In answer to this question I simply present the thesis that has ruled our thought throughout these later lectures: I believe we have a key to all the essentials of churchmanship in the relations between God, man, and the world which many of us know in public worship.

The most obvious rift in Western Christendom is of course that which has opened between Catholicism and Protestantism. I know that the situation is confused: that there are Catholic elements in Protestantism as there are Protestant elements in Catholicism, and that there is more than one church besides that of Rome which calls itself Catholic. For myself, I believe that the Protestant is the Catholic Church in principle; but in this lecture I follow the usage of common speech in America and in speaking of the Catholic Church refer only to the Roman Catholic.

The Catholic-Protestant rift is fortunately not absolute. There are even hopeful signs that it is lessening at certain levels.

For a long time the two groups in this country and elsewhere, though not everywhere, have co-operated in social services. Representatives of the two meet at conferences on social work and share each other's plans. The telephone wires between the settlement houses of the two in the congested districts of our cities are kept busy by frequent interchange of question and information. But this is rather an expression of civic responsibility and camaraderie than of anything ecclesiastical. It is a mingling of the waters of the two streams in the bay. It has simply nothing to do with sources. It does not affect the water of either stream; it does not alter their courses for better or worse.

Much more significant is the new theological interchange. In the Catholic international quarterly review, *Unitas,* and in many another Catholic journal, the events which mark the progress of Protestant ecumenicity are faithfully recorded. Even this reportorial interest is something new under the sun. But even more impressive are the Catholic studies of themes proposed by the Protestant World Council of Churches. Some of the best critiques of the papers put forth by the Evanston Conference have come from Catholic pens; and at this very moment the leading Catholic divinity men in Europe are, on their own initiative, preparing papers on themes suggested by the Study Commission of the World Council. To say that this is something new under the sun is to put the matter feebly: this is a new sun in the sky. It suggests at least that there is new light on the possibility of communication at an intellectual level.

This means to me, as a person interested in theological education, that from now on divinity schools like Yale and Harvard will hardly be doing their part in closing the rift unless they expose their Protestant students, because they are Protestant, to the best contemporary Catholic theology. This teaching can conceivably be done by Protestant divines, but even here the old rule would seem to hold, that no Catholic can tell the truth about Protestantism and no Protestant the truth about Catholicism. It is hard to recognize the overtones in an orchestra unless one has played an instrument in it himself and trained his ear as a participant must. To Catholic harmonies the Catholic mind is best attuned. A visiting professor who is an authority in Catholic history, theology, liturgics, ethics, or any other Catholic study would seem to be able not only to make a positive contribution to the curriculum of the school but also to provide in his person and teaching a lane of communication which might presently become an avenue. One thing we know: the wall of noncommunication which has stood between the groups for four centuries has been productive of nothing so much as misunderstanding. It is about time to make a new departure.

The new attitude discoverable by these signs in various quarters is encouraging enough, but it is not to be inferred that the groups are coming together as yet in any vital part. Here the thesis of these lectures, that the essence of the church is to be found in corporate worship, is only too starkly illustrated. If Catholics do not find in Protestant worship the same relationships between God and man, and man and man, that they enjoy in their own, if the Catholic Christ has a different character from the Protestant Christ, one must say that they are two different religions and conclude that the basic oneness on which alone reunion is conceivable seems to be lacking. But I am not at all sure that different relationships are discoverable respectively in the two types of service. In fact I am quite sure that the relationships of the two are fundamentally the same. This at any rate is the question to which the two groups must address themselves in the mutual inquiries which now begin to seem feasible.

The Protestants we know best today regard the Catholic order of priesthood as a Christian one and Catholic services, apart from the implications and parallels of what they understand to be the doctrine of transubstantiation, as involving the same kinds of relationship, all under Christ, as their own.

Here we have undoubtedly departed from the attitude of our fathers when the night of the Escalade in Geneva, the St. Bartholomew's Day massacre in Paris, and the agonies of the Thirty Years' War still caused the memory to bleed. I hope that no angry retaliation for being repudiated themselves will cause Protestants to give up the generous spirit of recognition toward Catholics which accompanies their modernity—but this magnanimity on the part of one group does not make it possible for them to worship with another which feels it has good theological reasons for maintaining liturgical aloofness.

The attitude of Catholicism to Protestantism is clean-cut, logical, and understandable, even to those who cannot accept its premises. It begins with the idea that Protestant forms have not proved themselves as pointing to the true relationships between God and man, and man and man, which are at the heart of the Church of Christ. A good Catholic therefore cannot recognize those forms by participating with Protestants in worship.

The hope of the situation lies in the possibility that participation in wholly nonliturgical enterprises, such as theological conversations, may eventuate in understandings which will be the basis for actual ecclesiastical collaboration. There is what de Madariaga calls "too much church" encumbering us now. So many habits of thought, so many manners and customs, have grown from a secondary to a primary place in our church life as to have obscured the essentials of faith. It is to clearing away these unessentials and getting back to what is found in simple corporate worship—the God-man and the man-man relationships—that our theological conversations and other preliminary activities should be directed.

The rifts to which the lion's share of our Protestant attention is given today are those which separate from each other our various communions outside the Church of Rome.

Time was when this series of chasms seemed as broad and un-bridgeable as that between Catholicism and the rest of Christen-dom, but ecumenicity in our generation has given us more hope of closing it than the world has enjoyed since our divisions first began to be. I was going to say, since the Great Schism of 1052, because at no other time during the long interval have there been anything like the number of strands of reciprocity between Orthodoxy and the West that have been developed lately. It is not necessary to recite the gains in this area, since they are everywhere in evidence. The ending of the age of division and the coming of that of *rapprochement* is symbolized most no-tably in the formation of the many councils of churches at local levels, of the national councils in various countries, and the World Council of Churches (and the International Missionary Council) crowning all.

When one crosses to these from Catholic-Protestant relation-ships he feels he has traversed a watershed, for here the various communions do recognize each other as having their one Christ in common. They can and do worship together in nonsacra-mental ways (here and henceforward I use the adjective "sac-ramental" as pointing specifically to the Sacrament and not in the broader sense of the previous lectures): they acknowledge, in Christ, the same relationships between God and man, and man and man. This, if my lectures mean anything, is a matter of simply limitless significance. If any denomination acknowl-edges (as all do) that the realities and several relationships it finds in public worship constitute the essence of the church and if it recognizes these same real elements in the worship of other denominations, then in principle it proclaims itself and the others to be part of the same church, having the one essence in common. This is precisely what the members of the World

Council of Churches have done in announcing their "unity in Christ."

These churches have gone farther. As a corollary to their basic conviction that the essence of the church is Christ and the relationships he sets up, they are ready to say that these relationships can be expressed in more than one set of forms. The principle that uniformity is not necessary to unity, indeed that multiformity is necessary to the richest kind of unity, was underscored as far back as the Edinburgh Conference in 1937, when it was said of the terms "corporate union" and "organic unity":

> These terms are forbidding to many, as suggesting the ideal of a compact governmental union involving rigid uniformity. We do not so understand them, and none of us desires such uniformity. On the contrary, what we desire is the unity of a living organism, with the diversity characteristic of the members of a healthy body.

The ecumenical movement has done more than set this forth as a pretty saying. It has furnished living proof that diversity in the forms of worship apart from the Lord's Supper (which I mean to speak of presently) is not a hindrance to unity. The delegates to an ecumenical gathering returning home all tell the same story: the most moving parts of the conference were the services of worship, led by men of various communions and according to liturgies as various as they. It is an experience quite unforgettable, especially if you find yourself in the midst of it for the first time, to be singing "Now thank we all our God" and hear the person in the same pew on one side of you singing, "Nun danket alle Gott" and someone on the other side taking it up in the words, "Rendez graces au Seigneur." One Gospel, different languages—and you sense that there has been given you a deep discernment: the verbal languages are a symbol of the ecclesiastical languages, that is, the episcopal, presbyterial, congregational systems of form. And is not this singing together, though with different words, a promise that a way will be found to permit each person to use his own church forms within the one church? At any rate, within one conference there are many types of nonsacramental services available and set in such a milieu that in attending one of them a worshiper is not disloyal to his own communion. The privileges of all are open to each member of the conference. Though the services differ in form, they are each regarded as services of the whole. Seen in the long perspective of post-Reformation church history this is something new: at least some of our fathers would have been surprised to have had such proof given them that in nonsacramental worship multiformity can be made to serve unity. Today it is taken for granted that in the "coming great church," if ever it comes, there will be many forms of nonsacramental worship.

Let us stop here long enough to take encouragement from this fact. It means that none of the communions in the ecumenical movement believe that matters of form—though obviously form of some sort cannot be dispensed with—are essential to worship. They are the modes, not the substance. Here there is not too much church and too little faith. I believe that all would come near to defining the eternal entities and eternal relationships as I have. Whatever the form used—Quaker silence or intoned liturgy or anything between or in any combination—the basis of Christian worship is the God of grace, the needy human soul, and other souls, all seen in the light that streams from the living Christ. Christians seem to agree that these realities and these relationships are to be found in each other's forms of worship, and because that is true I believe we may hope that the ecumenical movement has the nucleus of eternity at its heart.

Let us stay a little longer to mark that this situation by no means argues that all forms are equally good. It means that none of them are regarded as absolute. All are thrown into an emulative situation where, amidst living forces, the better may eventually displace the worse. When a set of ecclesiastical forms is locked within a denomination, where it is not susceptible of comparison with other forms used in other denominations, its existence is cut off from a chief source of life and growth: it is a tree with unpollenated blossoms. One of the most noticeable by-products of the ecumenical movement has been the improvement in liturgical practices through the entire denominational spectrum: churches that had allowed their forms to calcify too rigidly have learned from outside how and where to bring in needed suppleness, and those whose forms were conspicuously flabby have learned the value of having skeletal strength in the body.

Furthermore, when forms are thus placed in contiguity where they may come to enjoy a slow evolutionary maturing, it becomes necessary to have some standard, in order to recognize those which are better and those which are worse; and I do not hesitate to assert that to me this standard is that which is best oriented to the eternal realities to which I have so often referred. The forms which most instantly and unambiguously refer the attention to the judging and forgiving God, to the need for open-souledness toward Him and for open-handed helpfulness to one's fellow churchmen and the world, all epitomized and portrayed in the living Christ—those forms are best. Forms, on the contrary, which call attention to the celebrant of a rite or to the preacher or anything else less than God's grace and how it may bring salvation to men and mankind must slowly make their inferior way into disuse. The willingness of the various members of the ecumenical movement to enter into nonsacramental worship under each other's forms has brought all the forms under the fresh judgment of Christ.

It would seem to me that in the area of nonsacramental worship the members of the World Council of Churches and of other similar councils have discovered a divine chart for guidance through a plurality of forms to unity in fact.

1. They begin with the idea that the matter of most importance in the church is Christ and the relationships he calls into being.

2. They accept the fact that there are various forms that point toward him.

3. Though to each of them the forms used in his own communion seem to point more directly to Christ and what he desires among his people than the forms of other communions, they do not rule out those other forms as foreign to Christ's church.

4. They therefore are able to enter into each other's forms, finding the essentials there, more or less well expressed, and when they do so they do for the moment achieve unity—worshiping one God in one Christ, one Holy Spirit making them one people.

Why cannot this same course be followed in areas other than that of nonsacramental worship?

18. SACRAMENTAL WORSHIP AT THE ECUMENICAL LEVEL

WHERE FORM OBSCURES ESSENCE

Why cannot the course taken in nonsacramental worship be followed for the Sacrament itself? Why, at ecumenical gatherings, do the members of some communions feel they must go off by themselves for the Lord's Supper and not participate with the rest? Why do they not seem able to enter into each other's forms at this point?

This action on the part of some is not, as it has seemed to others, intended to be a liturgical insult to the rest of the church, but is the result simply of the belief that the rite of communion is a symbol of unity, which ought not to be entered into with those to whom one is not actually united. Better a seeming insult than an actual liturgical lie. The idea is that people who are not united should not by communicating at the same table say that they are.

But is it true that only people who are united should communicate at the Lord's Supper? The answer is an unqualified *yes* provided it is understood that that which unites them is the Lord himself. They are not necessarily united by their politics or their language or anything other than the living Christ. Those who eat the bread and drink the cup at the same table declare themselves to be in the relationship to God and each other of which Christ is the veritable personification. This is the focal point of their unity.

It is from this angle that the practice of making one's communion only among one's fellow denominationalists and not inviting other Christians to join in should be examined. Is it right to make the service of Holy Communion a sign not only of unity in Christ but also of general church unity, including the unity of ecclesiastical organization?

The psychiatrists may wish to state here what none of us will probably deny, that the business of going apart with like-minded people in a mood of exclusiveness may and often does represent a subliminal hunger for status over against the rest of the world. When it does, it is surely poles apart from the mind of Christ. But this is a matter to be considered by students of mental life, and not here. Our question is simply whether the exclusive communion-making which we often see in the ecumenical movement, and which constitutes one of the most difficult of its problems, is fitting from the point of view of Christian thought.

The reason this practice is an evil one is that it offends against the ends of Christian worship. Note that the situation here is quite different from that which Rome sees. Rome is uncertain whether the Christ of the non-Roman communions is really the same as that of Rome, that is, whether this is the true Christ and whether the relationships he elicits are the true Christian relationships. But the churches we are now speaking of are participants in the ecumenical movement. They have already declared that they are one in Christ and—a matter of critical import—they have actually worshiped together, supporting their declaration with action. True, their common worship is non-sacramental, but surely it is just as liturgically deceitful for people who are not united in Christ to worship together non-sacramentally as sacramentally. Is the Christ of the sacrament different from Christ as we meet him in other worship? Is the relation of God to man different there, or that of man to man? The only difference between the nonsacramental and the sacramental service is one of form: in the one, intellectual symbols like words are used for the most part, and in the other the materials of bread and wine, used and ordained by Christ himself—but both services are Christ's. There is no difference in essence between the two. If people are not united in him, they cannot worship Christianly in any corporate way.

The purpose of sacramental worship is to give souls a concrete medium for communion with Christ and with each other. This is according to Scripture and the seasoned understanding of the pious. To try to make it something more than that, to *use* it to advertise organizational church unity also, is to use Christ and human souls in a way which ruins the fundamental relationships of worship. It makes man and not God the master of the feast. All Christian worship implicitly proclaims union in Christ because it is directed to him: to try to make one particular type proclaim more than this is to make it less than Christian worship. Worship is worship. To use this kind of worship to signify this, and that kind of worship to signify that, is to make it a means and not the end that it is.

Keeping the service at the Lord's Table sacrosanct as a service of Holy Communion with Christ in which there is a meeting between God and the soul and other souls, and which is not intended to carry any other implication, provides at least three considerations in respect of forms.

1. The Lord's Supper as pure worship emphasizes the secondary (though indispensable) place of forms. While making use of a material medium for communication, it exalts not the medium but those whom the medium links together—God, who communicates Himself to His people, and the people, who in response communicate themselves to God and each other.

One of our great churches defines as necessities in a service of Holy Communion the use of the elements of bread and wine and the inclusion of

    a. A Prayer of Consecration, embodying the words and acts of our Lord in the Institution of the Sacrament, an Offering, an Invocation of the Holy Spirit, and a Thanksgiving,

    b. The Lord's Prayer, and

    c. The Apostles' Creed or the Nicene Creed as the symbol of the faith and unity of the Holy Catholic Church.

These are undoubtedly good historical forms for use in the Sacrament, and I have in fact singled them out for this reason, in order to intensify the contrast between the essence of the Sacrament and even good legislation regarding it. When a set of rubrics of this sort is put forth as *a* proper standard to follow, they have their perfect place, but the danger is that they will be taken as absolutes from which there can be no Christian deviation. This is to put Christ in a bed of Procrustes. In this day of ecumenicity, should not every good order, either within itself or in the general approach made by the communion to its total liturgical legislation, carry its badge of relativity? The deeply essential realities of the Holy Communion—God sacrificing Himself, man responding in contrition and love—may surely be expressed at the Holy Table in more than one way.

But this leads to a second consideration.

2. If communion may be expressed in more than one form, intercommunion is at least possible.

As a matter of fact most communions today accept more than one form among their own communicants. On the next Sunday morning that the Lord's Supper is laid in the Methodist Church there will be a deep-felt unity in the forty thousand congregations because it will be a unity in Christ, but more than one form will be used. The Book of Worship invites the people to communicate under either one of two forms. In less connectional churches many more than two forms will be used. Variety of form is indeed the rule. In few churches, even the most ultramontane, is it believed that Christ's institution was so specific as to fix the very syllables of the rite. The obligation resting on the church is merely generic, leaving choice open within limits. I do not happen to know any Western theologian, for instance, who holds either that the bread must be leavened or that it must not be leavened. The principle of variety in form does not vitiate the principle of unity in Christ. People in the same church can and do communicate under various forms.

And so enters intercommunion as a possibility, so far as forms are concerned, for if Christ can be found in more than one form, as proved by the experience within one's own church, it follows that he may be found within forms used in other churches.

In fact, given that the churches of the ecumenical movement have already discovered Christ in each other, it would seem to follow that Christ would surely be found by the various members in each other's Sacrament. That is, there should be as much reciprocity as possible at altars of the various communions and as little as possible of the fencing of tables against persons of other denominations in the movement. If Christ can be found in more than one form, is it not even something of a betrayal of our love for him never to look for him outside our own form? Christ can be separated from us in his fullness by too much church.

Intercommunion permits a comparison and so an improvement of form against the background of the eternal standard; and intercommunion, being generous, gracious, welcoming, approximates more closely to the mind of Christ and the relationships in Christ, and so does a better work of symbolization than does exclusion.

This position, when it is out-and-out, thoroughgoing, completely unself-centered, is, I believe, the truly Protestant one. Churches that hold to it have as logical a position as that which characterizes Catholicism. They take it as having been proved that the forms used by the other members of the ecumenical movement—including the sacramental forms—are genuinely designed to witness to the relationships between God and man, and man and man, which are declared in their own. They therefore conceive it as their duty to seek Christ in all of them without giving up their personal preference for and adherence to their own; and for this breadth of regard—this magnanimity in Christ—they have an ample and clear theological foundation.

3. If intercommunion among those who accept Christ as Lord rests on a solid foundation, it would seem to follow that in the church which is coming *in spe* there would and should be as many, and the same, forms of communion as there are today in the various denominations. Only so can people enjoy the forms which, since they are the most familiar, are likely to be the most meaningful, and yet belong to a church sufficiently catholic to include all.

In that church there will surely be many ways to celebrate communion with Christ. If a member desires to communicate in only one kind, what should there be to prevent him? Will not the privilege be accorded him in at least one corner of the great church's domain? Or if he can communicate better entirely apart from the visible wafer and wine, as the Friends seem to do, will the church deny him the right? If he prefers to accept communion only at the hands of a priest ordained by a bishop in a historic line, ought the rest of us to say him nay? What is now intercommunion will, we trust, take the shape of multiformity of communion in tomorrow's church.

19. ORGANIZATION AT THE ECUMENICAL LEVEL

The Recognition of Each Other's "Orders"

Comparable to the nonrecognition of each other's sacramental worship on the part of some denominations is the nonrecognition of each other's orders of ministry. It is part of the nonrecognition of each other's total organization and government. But given the fact that the various members of the ecumenical movement believe and announce and demonstrate in nonsacramental worship that they are one in Christ, how can they fail to recognize each other's structures as parts of Christ's church?

As a matter of fact most of them do, though not all. Some do not accept letters of dismissal and recommendation from other communions. Eastern Orthodoxy takes the position that other groups have separated from it and in so doing have separated themselves from the One, Holy, Catholic, and Apostolic Church. There is then only one way for them to recover unity— to return to the bosom of that church. Under these circumstances that church recognizes no politically organized church (to use the adverb in its earlier and good sense) outside itself. Yet there is a principle of freedom within Orthodoxy which expresses itself at some points in plurality of forms. One hopes that some formula may be discovered which will permit the Eastern Church to recognize still other forms.

All must come to see that polities—that is, types of organization—though indispensable, are yet forms and are therefore not of the essence of the church.

A corollary of this is that Christ may be extolled in more polities than one. Already there are different polities to be found within each of the larger communions. In the Protestant Episcopal communion there are churches in New England if not elsewhere which are just as autonomous as Congregational churches—not in the mythical sense of Congregationalism as completely independent of the *koinonia,* but in the true sense, which unites autonomy and fellowship. In the Congregational Christian domain, now a part of the United Church of Christ, there is at least one enclave as presbyterian in organization as John Calvin's Geneva. And there are spots in Presbyterianism where offices are constitutionally set up which are as episcopal as the principle of combining authority with position can make them. This is true usually in all but name, but in Hungary even the name of bishop is assigned to the chief presbyter. The Church of South India is built upon the idea that the several polities *are* therein united: the leaders believe that their church is congregational, episcopal, and presbyterian.

It is said that when polities are brought together the fusion must be such that one of them dominates. Critics say, for instance, that to all intents and purposes the United Church of Canada is essentially presbyterian and the Church of India essentially episcopal. Others deny these allegations. I do not see any reason why under a constitution it may not be agreed upon that one polity will rule at one point, another at another, all with a kind of veto power on the others, so that none can be said to control.

The Archbishop of Canterbury made a most interesting proposal a few years ago: that the nonepiscopal churches should take episcopacy into their systems and, as it were, try it out, being ready to be led by the Spirit in the process. Now I believe that most of the nonepiscopal denominations of broad gauge would be glad to take episcopacy into their systems, but they cannot do so and should not be asked to do so if this means excluding the nonepiscopal elements from their systems. It is imaginable, for instance (though just barely), that a Congregational conference or a Presbyterian synod, or several of them, in this country (as has been done elsewhere and is now proposed for Britain) might desire to have its chief office-bearer consecrated in an episcopal line. If this were the case, I think that the rest of us should take no exception to the procedure provided it did not follow that we should all be compelled, as members of sister conferences or synods of the same communion, to do the same thing or no longer be recognized as part of the same church. There are many Christians who have conscientious scruples against living under an episcopate, and we should want always to leave room for such people in any ecumenical system. I can understand why those who believe that congregationalism, episcopacy, or presbyterianism is part of the very *esse* of the Christian Church cannot afford theologically to see their polity polluted by either of the other two, but I do not expect to find the great-souled ecumenical Christian such as the churches are beginning to produce today, the man or the woman who has come to respect, though he cannot accept, church structures loved by his friends, yoked to a theology that will forbid plurality of polities within the one church.

Let me ask you to take up our yardstick again: what are the eternities you find in corporate worship in Christ's presence? You find God, you find yourself, you find your brother man— or if you do not, go thy way; first be reconciled to thy brother, and then come and offer thy gift. These you find there, but do you find episcopacy, presbyterianism, congregationalism? Are these names registered in heaven? I believe with all my heart that these forms have been and are necessary in history, but they seem of a quite secondary quality when compared with the deathless partners in worship, God and the soul and other souls. It is not that Christ does not belong to any of these polities: it is that he belongs to all.

20. FAITH AND ORDER

The Basic Necessities

The churches which are members of the ecumenical movement share each other's nonsacramental worship. They can do so because they believe themselves and have declared themselves one in Christ. But if they are one in Christ, if our argument has weight, they should also share in sacramental worship and recognize each other's organized life in every way consistent with their loyalty to Christ. This kind of intercommunion and mutual acknowledgment is far from being church union. But that too is adumbrated in being one in Christ.

When a congregation is at worship it is for the time being united, whether the worship be nonsacramental or sacramental. Those who think that sensitive worshipers can leave those services and go back with light heart to their own denominational separateness have never entered into the reality of the situation. They do not know how souls are drawn together by the grace of Christ and how it hurts, the service being ended, to see one's fellow Christians, with whom one has been for the moment united, going off into segregation again. If Christian services, sacramental and otherwise, are the celebration of Christ's presence, they must also register dedication on the part of the worshipers, to make their union in him cover the whole of their church life. A thought or two, therefore, concerning the church which is to be, especially in its relationship to forms, will not be amiss.

It has already been indicated that within the one church there may and should be plurality in forms. The declaration of the Edinburgh Conference, quoted previously, is to this effect. I cannot, however, conceive a church in which there is not fundamental unity in faith and in order. By faith I mean the believing loyalty which holds souls to God and to each other, and by order I mean the relationships that faith engenders. There will surely be both faith and order undivided in the One Church, as there will be faith and order in heaven.

Let us first speak of *order*. Here sharp differentiation is to be made between order and organization. The latter is a moment of polity, as I have been rather narrowly defining the latter. In

the report of the Oberlin Conference of 1957 on the Nature of
the Unity We Seek, order is called the visible means by which
God continues His church in being, and organization the tran-
sitory forms which come and go within historical change. It is
impossible for me to see how the church, in order to carry out
its mission, in order to be its apostolic self, can get along without congregations. These (in my thought at least) belong to
the realm of order. They may be organized in one way or another, in most lavish plurality, but they must continue to be.
Presbyterians believe or should, I think, believe that the church,
in order to be its apostolic self, cannot get along without elders,
and Episcopalians that it cannot do without bishops. These are
deep beliefs.

Let us then take them for granted and say with the World
Council of Churches that in any ecumenical plan there must
be congregations, there must be presbyters or leaders of congregations, and there must be episcopal leaders of leaders, shepherds of shepherds.

A bishop remains a bishop in episcopal order (though not
necessarily in succession) in spite of the many different ways
of organization in which he may relate himself to his priests and
ministers and in general to his whole diocese. He may have ap-
pointive power in one parish, but in another there may be a
permanent pastor who is as unsusceptible to episcopal removal
as he is sometimes impervious to episcopal advice. Under one
order there may be more than one type of relationship—even
more than one type of polity, for the status of the permanent
pastor is in fact as congregational as John Cotton could have
made it. The bishop is a bishop in spite of all differences
in organization which may be introduced. Similarly a presbytery, an assembly of elders, may be related to the churches
in many different ways of organization. There are differences in

the relationships at this point among all the Reformed Churches in the various countries of Europe. The ways of Scotland do not necessarily hold in Philadelphia, or in Toronto. But presbyteries everywhere are charged with keeping God's church in being in all the ways of good supervision. They are an order, though they may carry out their work in one manner of organization or another.

Likewise a congregation within a congregational system may be related to its association, conference, synod, or union in more than one way. I have mentioned one conference in this country which is presbyterian in its relationships; there are many others like it on the mission field. These do not cease to have standing as congregational-type congregations, for they continue to be recognized by the communion as congregations "congregated by Christ": they are companies of people dedicated to doing the things of Christ, whatever be their relationships to their denomination according to written or unwritten constitutions.

The place of the permanent pastor may some day be eliminated by those who believe it inconsistent with the general Episcopal idea, as may be the presbyterial elements in Congregationalism by those who see inconsistencies there—as indeed may be all plurality of organization in any particular ordered communion—but for the moment this hobgoblin of little minds does not prevail. There are various organizations within the several orders, and they seem to be getting along very well.

The so-called "Greenwich Plan" for a united church in the United States is the first one to be laid before American Christendom which avails itself of the principle that there may be, and let us say that in the completely united church there must be, a plurality of all the polities within the one order. It is designed for denominations that recognize or can come to recognize each other's ministries. It takes account of and builds upon the fact that the organizations in the major communions of the country have come to resemble each other. Each denomination has local churches, county bodies of churches or something corresponding, state bodies or something similar of the same size, and national bodies; and for the local churches there are ministers and for the state and national bodies office-bearers who, whether they are called bishops or not, possess episcopal functions. Their conception of order, in a word, is similar.

Here, however, the similarity ends. The relations between the various parts, the ecclesiastical bodies and the office-bearers, differ from communion to communion. In the Presbyterian denominations the presbytery, or "county body" of my description, has a different relation to its congregations from that of a similar body in the non-Presbyterian denominations. So in an episcopal system the bishop has not the same constitutional relation to the churches of the diocese that the corresponding office-bearer of another denomination has. Indeed there are bishops in different *episcopal* systems whose authorities differ.

The proposal of the "Greenwich Plan" is to unite what I have called the orders and to continue, at least at the beginning, the various types of organization. Here in Connecticut, for instance, for purposes of ecclesiastical legislation, there would no longer be a Baptist Association, a Congregational Conference, an Episcopal Convention, a Methodist Conference, and so on. These would be united in one meeting of the representatives of the Church of Christ in Connecticut. This body would take action on behalf of all the churches, but those churches would relate themselves to that action variously—exactly as they do now. The Congregational churches would treat it congregationally, the Presbyterian presbyterially, and the Episcopal episcopally. They would feel that it had different degrees of authority. The whole would be set forth constitutionally, with provision made for change of status, on long-term notice, if a church wished to pass, for instance, from a congregational relationship to the legislative body to a more highly connectional one, or vice versa.

This will seem to some a rather complicated arrangement until it is remembered that the churches in all denominations today are practically related to their state legislative bodies, in spite of all particular theories of polity, in very similar ways. The dynamics of American social life enforce this similarity. "Most of our churches," says the Oberlin report, ". . . whether of episcopal, presbyterial, or congregational polity—are speaking the same language when they come to discuss the place of authority in the church."

On the side of church administration, to draw our illustration again from Connecticut, the offices of Baptist Superintendent, Congregational Superintendent, Episcopal Bishop, Methodist Bishop, and corresponding office-bearers would be united. Ideally there would be one bishop of the Church of Christ in Connecticut, but he would be related to the ministers and churches of the state in all the several ways in which the various offices to be united are now related to them. The churches of the congregational type would go to him as a father in God for counsel and advice, those of the presbyterial type would go to him also as the chief executive of a constitutional court, and those of the episcopal type as to one who was responsible for their ordination or for the confirmation of the people in their parish. He would come quickly to have what might be called liturgical status among all groups: he would be a natural person to represent the church inside and outside the ecclesiastical enclave.

Now I do not believe that this or any plan like it will gain much headway for a hundred years. The Greenwich Plan itself calls for radical revision, especially in its description of the nature of the church. Perhaps something like this will be tried out on a small scale somewhere. I hope so. I have described it at some length here simply because I believe that it is based upon sound theoretical foundations and therefore deserves to succeed. The Greenwich Plan was actually reviewed by one of the committees that prepared for the Oberlin Conference, but that group found the more general ecumenical questions which were brought into focus by it so absorbing of time and interest that they could not take up at any length the specific type of pluralism which is the genius of it.

In any case, if those interested in the ecumenical movement are to be divided into three classes, (1) those who believe that their church polity is the only true type and try to draw all others into it, (2) those who believe their type is a persistent and inextinguishable one but are disposed to think that others may be best for other types of people, and (3) those who think that polity is unimportant and unnecessary, I can wish that the middle group may come to the fore with some creative planning. The third group is, I think, negligible. We tend to be dominated by the first group because of the charity of the rest of us. Every communion wants to hold together; and if within a denomination there is a considerable body that advertises that the communion will be broken if any recognition of other orders is made, the others tend to suppress their own hopes and allow the whole group to be frozen to its own past. One of the virtues of the early leadership in the Church of South India was that the forward-looking men in the several communions were courageous enough to choose to ally themselves with each other for the march into the future, even at the expense of breaking with the overconservative in their own communions.

There is one more area in which there must be some degree of actual unity—the area of *faith*. Of this I need say little because I believe there is a consensus of thought among us. The faith that holds the church together is not a set of sentiments but a loving response to the God who in Christ has first loved us, a self-conscious love that binds us at once to God and to each other. Christian faith may be said to be the essential content of the mind of a congregation at the moment of public worship.

Here also there is possible a plurality within the unity. Speakers of English, as has been pointed out a thousand times, are a bit bedeviled by the fact that the word "faith" has two meanings: both *confidence* and a *system of religious belief*. In the church there can be only one kind of basic confidence, that which is found in the love that will not let us go. This is the source in whose ocean depths the life we owe, given back, becomes eternally richer, eternally fuller. Drinking of this, we love the brethren. In the church which is to be, systems of belief will be as many as they are in the great communions of today: there will be Barths and Tillichs, Calhouns and many others, and all their following. Within the circle of love, which begins with Christ as the center and runs out through all the radii of membership beyond the periphery of the church to all the needy people of the world, there will be a plurality of theological sectors. The oneness will be found in Jesus Christ, through whom God is bringing His church into unity. "Purity of heart," said Kierkegaard, "consists in willing one thing." In the purehearted church, that one thing will not be a system of theology, however important some system of theology must be, but it will be Jesus Christ.

What does the living Christ ask of those who *worship* in his name? That is the question asked by these lectures.

Index